Who's Your Bubba?

Publisher: Jim Hoskins

Production Manager: Gina Cooke

Cover Designer: Lauren Smith

Copyeditor: Ellen Falk

Proofreader: Publication Services

Library of Congress Cataloging-in-Publication Data

Bechtol, T. (Terryl)
Who's Your Bubba? : the best of T. Bubba Bechtol / Terryl Bechtol.
p. cm.
ISBN 978-1-931644-56-3 (pbk.)
1. Bechtol, T. (Terryl) 2. Comedians—United States—Biography. I. Title.
PN2287.B396A3 2007
792.702'8092—dc22
[B]
2007011009

Who's Your Bubba?

The Best of T. Bubba Bechtol

MAXIMUM PRESS
605 Silverthorn Road
Gulf Breeze, FL 32561
(850) 934-0819
www.maxpress.com

Dedication

To the women in my life... all the role models I have had in my life have been female.

To my teachers, Ms. Anderson, Ms. Taconi, Ms. Alexander, Ms. Tina and Dr. Lady Ruth Carter... thank you.

To my fearless mother, Winona Leah Walker Bechtol Bryant, who raised five children by herself, and to the woman I will die with, Tarsha Marie, aka 'Lishous... thank you all for loving me in spite of my many faults.

With love,

James Terryl "T. Bubba" Bechtol, CSP

T. Bubba doing his thing at the Grand Ole Opry.

Hey Y'all...

I dun hooked up to the Internet!
Come visit me at:

TBubbaFun.com

We'll have a
good time...

Just because you
bought this book, you
get a **Secret Bubba Password**
to use at the Web Site:

298982

Come check it out!

And listen... thanks for buying
my book.

Table of Contents

★ ★ ★

★ ★ ★

CHAPTER 1

IGMOS

"IGMO" is a cross between "Ignorant" and "Moron." I made up this word thirty years ago to describe people who sometimes act like they are... not so bright. I would never call anyone stupid—I'm too nice to do that—but I will call someone an IGMO. When I use this word at work, I walk away smiling to myself because they have no idea of what I'm talking about. IGMOs are otherwise normal people that do and say the dumbest things at times. They are everywhere, and I like to point them out. I've included IGMO sections on every comedy album I have ever done, so I thought a study of IGMOs would be a good place to start this book.

Aunt Betty's Bill

My Aunt Betty died over seven years ago and a credit card company is still sending her bills. She left the little pink house on Panferio to me, where I now live. Ever since, I have just been throwing the bills away as they have continued to come. When I did Aunt Betty's estate, I had notified everyone of her death, so I wasn't worried about it. Last week I opened

My Aunt Betty.

one of the bills just to see why they were still sending her mail. I discovered that they had been billing her for their monthly service charge and an annual fee on a zero balance! With several years' worth of fees and late charges on them, the bill was $203.44. I was amazed, so I called the number on the bill in New York, and the conversation went something like this:

"Hello, this is Bubba Bechtol, I am calling to tell you that Ms. Betty Simon died years ago."

The credit card person said, "The account was never closed and the late fees and charges still apply."

"Maybe you should turn it over to Collections," I said with a wicked grin on my face that she couldn't see.

"Well, Mr. Bubba" (she missed the last name totally), "since it is years past due, I am sure it already has been."

I couldn't believe it, so I carried on with, "So, what will they do when they find out she is dead?"

"Either report her account to the frauds division, or report her to the credit bureau... maybe both!" she said in a nasty tone.

I had to hold myself to keep from laughing out loud in the phone. I said, "Do you think God will be mad at her?"

"Uh, excuse me, what did you say?" she asked.

"Did you just get what I was telling you... the part about her being dead?"

"Sir, you'll have to speak to my supervisor!" And with that I waited for the higher authority!

When Ms. Supervisor came on the phone, she said, "Sir, what seems to be the problem?"

I said, "I'm calling you to tell you that Betty Simon died years ago and I have not heard from her since the day she died!"

Without skipping a beat she said, "Well, the account was never closed and the late fees and charges still apply."

I bit my lip to maintain a straight face and said, "Do you want to collect from her estate?"

This one slowed the "higher authority" down a bit and she stammered, "Are you her lawyer or something?"

I said, "No, I'm her nephew, Bubba."

Then she said, "Well Sir, could you fax us a certificate of death?"

I said, "Sure, I will fax you the actual copy of the last fax I sent you years ago!"

She gave me the fax number and said, "We are just not set up in this department to handle death!"

I said, "I can understand that, I'm not either!"

This totally confused her and to my astonishment she said again, "Well, the late fees and charges still apply, as far as we are concerned!"

I then said, "Well would you like her new billing address? You could just continue to send her bills, I'm sure she wouldn't mind! As a matter of fact, I can assure you that it won't bother her a bit." I waited.

She actually said, "Well, fine, what is it?" I slowly said into the phone, "It is Rose Lawn Cemetery, plot 166, number 22, 2902 Gulf Breeze Parkway, Gulf Breeze, Florida 32501."

I waited with great anticipation, and sure enough she came back with, "Sir, that's a cemetery!"

I shouted into the phone, "Yes it is... what do *you* do with dead people up in New York City?!!"

All I heard was a click. I hope I get another bill from these IGMOs, but I bet I don't!

Just thought you'd like to know...

4 Who's Your Bubba? (TBubbaFun.com)

IGMO Signs

The more I travel, the more "IGMO signs" I see! Here are a few I have seen or people have sent to me recently. It makes me wonder if people that put these signs up ever read them; but then, if they did, we would not be able to laugh at them.

- Sign in a little restaurant in Franklin, Tennesee: "WE ARE OPEN SEVEN DAYS A WEEK, AND ON WEEKENDS." This owner will never catch up—he's on a nine-day week!!

- Sign in a tattoo shop in Daytona Beach, Florida: "TATTOOS WHILE YOU WAIT!" Well, how else you gonna do that? It's hard to drop your arm off and pick it up on Friday.

- Sign on the grounds of Forrest Glenn Prep School in Vermont: "NO TRESPASSING WITHOUT PERMISSION." Those Northerners can get uppity about permission!

- Sign at Health Department in Pensacola, Florida: "MENTAL HEALTH PREVENTION CENTER." I been there and it works!!

- Saw this sign on an automatic restroom hand dryer in a Mapco Station in Nashville, Tennessee: "DO NOT OPERATE WITH WET HANDS." Now if my hands are dry, I don't need the stupid thing. What does that mean, anyway?

- Sign in Memorial Gardens at Mystic Seaport, Connecticut: "PERSONS ARE PROHIBITED FROM PICKING FLOWERS FROM ANY BUT THEIR OWN GRAVES." Now this one got me! Can't you see a dead person picking his own flowers from his final resting place? And Yankees make fun of the way Southerners talk!

Saw this sign on an automatic restroom hand dryer in a Mapco Station in Nashville, Tennessee:
"DO NOT OPERATE WITH WET HANDS."

- Sign in the Mirage Hotel, Las Vegas, Nevada: "GUESTS WILL PLEASE REGISTER COMPLAINTS AT THE PERSONNEL OFFICE ON THE SECOND FLOOR BETWEEN THE HOURS OF 9 AND 11 a.m." I loved it! There was NO personnel office on the second floor!

- Sign in a restaurant in Jackson Hole, Wyoming: "CUSTOMERS WHO FIND OUR WAITRESSES RUDE SHOULD SEE THE MANAGER!" I bet that would help a lot!

- In the Gulfport Memorial Hospital maternity ward in Gulfport, Mississippi: "NO CHILDREN ALLOWED." I wonder what they do with the babies? This inspired me to make my own sign so I got out my black magic marker and on the swinging door to the delivery room I wrote... PUSH, PUSH, PUSH!!

Just thought you'd like to know...

"Bless Your Heart... "

For thirty years now, I have loved explaining the meaning of "Bless Your Heart." You see, in the Southland, you can say anything you want to about anyone, be just as vile and ugly as you want to be, and as long as you say, "Bless Your Heart" at the end, all is well. It just tempers the language and puts it all in perspective. Thirty years ago while on the speaking tour, I used this term a lot to avenge those people that thought they were smarter than us Southern Folk.

Of course, Northerners and other invaders think we are actually blessing them and that makes it all the more fun. Like when we say, "You know, it's amazing. Even though she had that baby just seven months after she was married, it weighed in at a full ten pounds... bless her heart!" Or, "You know, that boy is as ugly as a bucket full of armpits... bless his heart!" And, the reply, "Well, he can't help it, he looks just like his momma... bless her heart, too!"

I was thinking about this last week when I played golf with a man that just moved here from Iowa and was complaining that he couldn't find any good sweet corn bread in any of the restaurants. I told him, "Well, you know Bubba, you lived there thirty-three years, you'd think your wife would have found a recipe in all that time and learned to make it... bless her heart!" He had that look a man has that has just painted a wall, went to work, came home, and his son wrote on it, "I Love You Dad" with a purple Magic Marker! But, he ain't none too smart... bless his little Iowa corn bread heart!

Then his boss that was also from "up nawth" chimed in with, "Yeah, it's hard to find a great golf course here as well." I replied, "It must be different for you, I'm sure, with all the different rules and such, cause we don't usually use a tee in the middle of the fairway like you did on that last hole... bless your heart!" He had very little to say for the rest of the game.

Don't get me wrong. I love people from these places; I even married one. But we got her nearly 'bout southernized, cause she is saying "y'all," "fixin to," and "come on down" all the time now. While she never had any accent at all, cause her momma insisted on proper annunciation, she did use strange words like "these ones?" "I'll run you over" instead of "I'll run over you!" and "youse." She is now "cutting the light off," "carrying me to the Dr.," and yesterday I heard her say "yonder!" She has dumped most of her northern words for proper English these days. The smart ones adapt when they arrive... bless their hearts!

However, the people that I just want to slap the tar out of are the Southern-born natives that are ashamed of the way they talk and even go to "diction school" to learn not to talk like they was raised. My old buddy, Lewis Grizzard, said once that a movie director had called to tell him they were going to "pass on his screen test" because his dialect was "too Southern." After making an unfortunate mention about the director's parents' not being legally married when he was born and calling him a "po-born male chicken sucker," Lewis yelled into the phone, "Bubba, you can kiss my ass, cause it's impossible to be too Southern!" I hope these people that don't want to carry on the tradition of our fine Southern language wind up

T. Bubba clowning with country music legend Garth Brooks.

working next to a Pakistani in a 7-11 someplace saying, "Pak six and I C cream is all for you?"

It's a poor frog that won't croak about his own pond, and I feel that way about everyone wherever they are from. My buddy Buster told me one day, "Bubba, don't never embarrass a man and ask him where he from. If he's from the 'Redneck Riviera,' he'll tell you. If he ain't, don't make him feel inferior by explaining to you where he really is from!" I love Buster; he can't help being ugly, but he could have stayed at home... bless his heart!

Just thought you'd like to know...

Tourons

I have loved getting to know the different people that service our tourist industry—the waiters and waitress types, the bartenders, and folks that work on Pensacola Beach aka "Bubba's Beach"—the heart of the Red Neck Riviera on the beautiful Gulf Coast of Florida.

Hanging out at different restaurants and bars and just listening is beyond belief! We get a lot of "tourons" here. Turons are a cross between "tourist" and "morons." Turons are akin to IGMOs in the worst way.

I cannot believe the questions and statements that some people ask.

I was in the Sun Ray last night and a woman came in and ordered a "beef and bean burrito." She then asked, ''Is there any meat in that?'' Marga the waitress is no fool, only a few months away from her PhD in psychology (no joke)... She just looked the other way and waited for the woman to discover her mistake. She did not. Marga made the mistake of looking at me and I just said, "Tell her we can just grind up the hooves, it will still be beef, but no meat!"

A lady walked up to Lisa, the bartender, and ordered a "gin and tonic." When Lisa gave it to her, she looked at it and said, "No, I want a gin and tonic." Lisa said, "Lady, this a gin and tonic." The lady looked right at her and asked, "Just what is in a gin and tonic, anyway?"

Lisa looked her right in her eyes and said, very slowly, "Ginnnnnnn and Tonnnnnic!!!" I fell off my stool laughing and didn't stop until the lady left the bar.

They have to be nice... I don't. I think when people are acting stupid, if you don't laugh at them, it spreads and what kind of world would we have then?

"Just what is in a gin and tonic, anyway?"
Lisa looked her right in her eyes and said,
very slowly, "Ginnnnnnn and Tonnnnnic!!!"

I was getting breakfast one morning at the Sun Deck. I love their breakfast; it is nearly like home and the grease is free. I thought that I would get cute and ordered two eggs, bacon, home fries, and coffee. I told the waitress, "I want one egg over light and one scrambled!" She did just that, and when she served it to me, I looked at it a long time and then looked up at her and said, "You scrambled the wrong one!" She looked at it, looked at me (I had managed to keep a very straight face), then turned the plate around and said, "There, Bubba, now you can eat the

T. Bubba and legendary country music vocalist Faith Hill—two Mississippi folks.

right one first!" It was the best breakfast I ate all year and we laughed about it for months!

Now when I go in and the place is packed, I order the same way, we do the same act, and she will bring me out two eggs in their shells and ask me, "Bubba, which one do you want scrambled?" I pick one and when the plate comes, I look very satisfied. I love it when the person sitting next to me just looks at me and wonders, "How does he know?"

I was at "Peg Leg Pete's" one night and a man at the next table asked for coffee with no cream. The waitress said, "We are out of cream; you will have to take it with no sugar!" It was scary! I don't think she lasted too long!

So here's to all the people that take care of the Tourons, the Yankees, and the IGMOs that ask those questions that make you just want to stab yourself in the eye to relieve the pain! Keep smiling, keep laughing, and keep me informed. I love it!

Just thought you'd like to know...

Sayings!

All over America we have "sayings." Some are distinctive to the area and some are national in meaning. We grow up with them. They become part of our language. We attach meanings to them, some of them quite serious.

I always found them a bit funny. Even as a child, I thought, "Why don't we say what we mean and not quote some stupid saying?" I began to cogitate over them and today find them quite funny. Here are a few "sayings" that are just not what we mean when we use them!

"You Can't Take It with You." This not true. It all depends on what "it" is. If it is your dark suit, not only can you take it with you, you can probably put some things in the pockets. You can take your money with you if you spend all you can, die broke, and give the rest to God. It just takes some planning!

"You Learn Something New Every Day." Actually, you learn something *old* every day. Just because it is new to you doesn't mean it's new. Other people already knew it, for sure.

"The Sky Is the Limit." Dumb! The sky never ends. The Earth is the limit; just ask any astronaut. If you dig a hole, you get more earth; you can't get more sky! The earth is the limit.

"Tomorrow Is Another Day." Scarlet was very distressed when she gave this to us in "Gone with The Wind." Actually, today is another day. Tomorrow never comes, for when it does, it is today. Best bar sign I ever saw said, "Free Beer Tomorrow." Get it? Huh, do you? Okay... then say it right!

"Nice Guys Finish Last." Not true. Studies have shown that on average, nice guys finish third in a field of six. Actually, short guys finish last in almost every study. "Big & Tall" guys finish first and women still seem to be crashing against the self-imagined "glass ceiling."

"If You Have Seen One, You've Seen Them All." This may be the dumbest one of all. This should be obvious. If you've seen one... you just saw one. You can only "see 'um all" if you see each and every one of them. No two things in the world are exactly alike. Not even identical twins. Another stupid maxim!

"Those Were the Days." NO, those were the nights. Think back, weren't the nights better? You have to work in the daytime. At night you went to parties, went sailing, danced, and drank. So from now on it is "Those Were the Nights" Okay?

"Life Is Short." Sorry. Life is not short. Everybody lives exactly as long as they are supposed to. It is written in the book of Bubba. Death, on the other hand, can be very short!

"What You Don't Know Won't Hurt You." Sure... why don't they ask John Lennon, John Kennedy, or Julius Caesar about that. What you don't know can kill, as a matter of fact.

"It Takes Two To Tango." This is just not true. One can tango by one's self; you will just look a bit stupid doing it.

"Things Have Got to Get Better. They Can't Get Any Worse." Whoever said this first had never been through a hurricane! They never had a toothache, and for sure they had never been married!

And finally, **"You Can't Have It Both Ways."** Sure you can. Sometimes I get it six different ways! It just depends on how well you know the other person and sometimes there is "only one way to do a thing."

Just thought you'd like to know...

IGMOs Are Everywhere

IGMOs are everywhere. They print up signs, make products to sell, preach from pulpits, and live on television commercials.

For instance, I have heard people say things that just make me want to slap them in front of their mommas and send them back to school. I hear it everywhere. Things like "Childproof"... there ain't no such thing as childproof. Bubba Jr. proved that before he was six years old. I got him one of those "unbreakable toys;" he used it to break all his other toys with! Nothing is childproof. The people who name toys that are IGMOS.

I heard a commercial the other day that said, "Synthetic Natural Gas." How can that be? If it is synthetic, it ain't natural. However, if you mess with synthetic gas, it might blow your natural head off!

The TV said last night, "Taped Live"... well, how else you gonna do that? Do you really think that they would tape a tape? It's all live in the beginning, then it's taped. Get a clue, ABC!

Bubba-Lishous said last night she was going to wear "Tight Slacks" to dinner. Huh? If they are tight then they ain't "slacks!" I don't wear tight anything. Spandex and Bubba don't go well together, regardless of color. When I put on a pair of stretch pants, brother... they ain't got a choice! 'Lishous is an IGMO about twice a week.

I was in the store yesterday and saw a "Ten-Ounce Pound Cake;" if it's ten ounces, it ain't a pound cake! We should sue them for false advertising and make them make a sixteen-ounce pound cake!

I read in the paper that over the Memorial Day weekend, several people were arrested that were "Legally Drunk"... well, kick me in the butt and call me darlin', there is no legal way to be really drunk! Drunk is all ille-

*I was in the store yesterday and saw a
"Ten-Ounce Pound Cake;" if it's ten ounces,
it ain't a pound cake!*

gal, ain't it? If you're "legally drunk," then you ain't drunk at all, that's the way I see it!

I heard someone say "British Fashion" the other day. There ain't no such thing! I have watched the British dress for over fifty years, and the only one that had any fashion is the man on the Beefeater Gin Bottle! After all, the British gave us Twiggy and Elton John; now there was a fashion gift to the world, wasn't it? Most British people look like their house was on fire when they dressed. Give me a break here! Most British are IGMOs.

Bubba-Lishous heard a radio commercial the other day that said, "All natural scientifically formulated." Even she said, "WHAT? If it's scientifically formulated, it ain't natural!" God is natural, man is scientific! Can't be both! I ain't gonna eat nothin' that is scientifically formulated, but I'll eat natural most of the time.

Finally, the one that gets me every time is "Same Difference." Only the biggest IGMOs use this term. They are the people that don't know they don't know. Same Difference makes about as much sense as Government Organization; it just don't exist in this world!

So say what you mean, and mean what you say. See what I'm saying here?

Just thought you'd like to know...

CHAPTER 2

Bubba Wonders

When I began to write for newspapers many years ago, I had to develop a new thought process. I began to "ponder" and to "wonder," and it became a new habit for me. I began to go out to the sand dunes and walk along the coastline and just ponder what to write about. People need to ponder more. It would be a better world.

Wondering!

I've been wondering. I like to wonder; it's easier than thinking and a lot easier than pondering. Pondering and thinking require some type of answer, but when you wonder, you don't have to come up with any answers.

I wonder about everything. I wonder what the first Bubba was thinking way back in time when he saw the first cow and said, "You know, I'm gonna squeeze those dangly things down there between her hind legs and drink whatever comes out!" Man, he was a brave Bubba!

I wonder who the first Bubba was that thought that white oval thing that came from a hen's butt looked like something to eat. Can you imagine? He stumbles across this nest of white things, the animal is squawking and clucking like she's scared to death, and he says, "Man, I'm gonna eat that thing that just dropped out of her butt!" I don't think he was brave, I think he was just hungry! Mighty hungry...

I wonder who the first Bubba was that thought that white oval thing that came from a hen's butt looked like something to eat.

I wonder if Jimmy Cracked Corn and he didn't care, then why did they write that song about him? Jimmy sounds like an IGMO to me; how stupid do you have to be to crack corn and not care! I don't care either way, and I'm even sorry I wondered about it now.

I wonder what you call a male ballerina? What do you call a male lady bug, a Male Lady Bug? And I wonder if the bug cares? I wonder also just why women are prone to never forget things that need forgetting.

And finally, if quizzes are quizzical, do you call tests... testicals? I don't; but then I don't care either.

Just thought you'd like to know...

Thoughts on Things

I have always wondered why we think thoughts. I think we think thoughts because if we didn't, we would never know when we are doing anything. If we didn't know when we were doing something, then nothing would ever get done on purpose.

Now, that would be a mixed-up crazy world, but I'd love to at least spend the night there!

T. Bubba and Drew Carey living large at the Super Bowl.

It is like time and space. God invented time and space, so everything wouldn't happen at once in the same place.

Therefore, I pondered on it this week and came up with some thoughts that are not too deep, but require just enough consideration to be incomplete.

I wonder why we call it bird seeds. Birds don't grow from them; I think we should I call them plant seeds for birds. Or wouldn't "bird grain" make more sense?

I wonder if you ever got amnesia, if you would remember it. I guess if someone actually left their heart in San Francisco and you found it, how would you get it back to the right person?

I know money can't make me happy; all I want is the chance to find out for myself.

The world doesn't make sense. If the world made sense, little boys would learn to ride bicycles side-saddle!

I saw a sign on a perfume desk in Dillard's that said, "Free Gift." Ain't all gifts free?

I saw another sign on the I-10 tunnel in Mobile that said, "All vehicles with flammable liquid must detour." Stupid sign; all vehicles carry flammable liquid. It's called gasoline!

I wonder if you told someone that they were gullible, if they would believe you.

If you teach a child to be nice to strangers, how is he ever going to drive a car in California?

I wonder if a turtle actually smells through his butt (and I understand they do), what a belch would smell like. I wonder if he smells his food before he eats it, and exactly how the turtle does do this, and how does he feel about it.

They say that God never makes mistakes. What about gnats, the duck-billed platypus, PMS, rude Yankees, politicians, fatness, snakes, and welfare, as we know it?

And finally, I wonder why my wife expects me to understand just why she loves me.

Just thought you'd like to know...

Bubba's Belly Button

The other day I was digging around in my belly button. I know that's a bit gross, but let's face it, you've done it too. I wondered what the stuff I got out of my belly button was. We call it "belly button lint." I don't have a lint filter in there, but I do have an agitator! I have no idea of how the stuff gets into my belly button and I sure don't want to know where it goes when I don't pick it out of there!

I pondered on what to use the stuff for. It's strong, it's clean, and it's fiber, so there must be some constructive use for it. I think the piece I pulled out was big enough to knit a bathing suit for a Baywatch girl... at least. Or you could string some together and save money on dental floss.

I wonder where it would send you if you smoked it? I think you could save it all up and in a year have enough to certify your entry into the "navel" academy! You could wet it and take it to Bobby D's to use as spitballs to hit the TV screens with on karaoke nights. I did that one night while Lishous was doing her DJ thing and by the end of the night you couldn't even see the screen. No one even noticed!

You could sell it to toy manufacturers for baby doll hair pieces. It could be good with liver and onions, or used in the outdoor grill to start the fire on your charcoal. If it has DNA in it, you could use it in court to convict serial killer belly dancers.

You could use it on fishing lures to attract fish and I bet the fish would love it! You could put it on the end of match sticks and have instant Q-tips. I could save it up for two years and make myself a Santa Claus beard for Christmas time.

There are a million ways to use it, I guess, but I just roll it up and feed it to our cat. The cat loves it, and it has given a totally new look to the fur balls she leaves for me on the tile floor in the middle of the night. Rolex, my dog, won't eat them; he's smarter than that. He can smell human skin all over it, and he tried the "skin" taste once and didn't like it. He does, however, like to eat them in the fur balls from the cat. So, I'm sure there is a dog/cat relationship there to help me with this belly button lint problem. Ain't animals wonderful? I know... I'm nuts.

Just thought you'd like to know...

Just Thinking

I been thinking. Sitting on a sand dune and thinking. I get on my motorcycle to ride and peruse the island and find a great spot to sit and think. I thought a lot faster yesterday when I sat on a cactus and had to have a stranger at the Circle K pull several needles out that I couldn't get to—but I've been thinking.

I hear things that are wrong or "almost right" and complete them. Sometimes I just think things up that come to me in a fit of thinking... Either way, it's thinking. Thinking is good. The only thing better than thinking is pondering. But pondering sometimes requires more thought and that leads to discussions with myself. People look at me funny when I do that, so I been just thinking...

I like to simplify things. Put them into little short sentences that make more sense. Here are a few for you to think about.

- God wants spiritual fruit, not religious nuts! I know cause he told me so.

- Manage your own morals. You can't manage others'... With the exception of your own children, don't even try.

- There is no "key" to a happy life. The door is always open.

- It is hard to misinterpret silence.

- Faith is the thing that causes you not to panic.

- Prayer is like calling home every day and talking to your mother. If you don't pray, you don't have a home.

- Flexible people are never bent out of shape.

- The heaviest load I know is a personal grudge.

- Nothing ever becomes real to you until you experience it, good or bad. Until then it is just imagined. If your imagination becomes real to you, this is called insanity!

- If you ever "dance with the devil in the pale moonlight," don't let him lead. Trust me on this one.

- We need more free speech that is worth listening to.

• And finally, diaper, spelled backwards, is repaid; think about it...

Just thought you'd like to know...

Ponderings from Bubba's Beach

I was sitting on a sand dune yesterday at Bubba's Beach and pondered. I like to think up things that have not been thought of yet. You know, like questions that should have been asked but have not been yet! It's a wonderful waste of time!

I wonder if you can cry underwater... and if you can, what would it sound like? I tried it yesterday but couldn't totally understand myself! I think maybe I did, but I'm not sure!

I pondered why bologna is round and white bread is square. I guess because if they were both round it would be a bologna burger—and that don't sound real "bon apple titer!" Why don't round pizzas come in round boxes? Is it because they wouldn't stack up as well? Weird, ain't it? I wonder if they were round, would it still be a "box?"

Why do Tourons (a cross between morons and tourists) here on Bubba's Beach go back into a roughed-up Gulf of Mexico right after they are told by the authorities to "get out because they could drown in the rip currents?" It is really hard to legislate against STUPID. You have a right to be

---

I pondered why bologna is round and
white bread is square.

STUPID in this country. You can ride a motorcycle without a helmet. You can leave your seatbelt unfastened. You can eat your ice cream from the same spoon you are feeding your dog with. You can smoke cigarettes until you die of painful cancer. There are all matters of things that you have a right to be STUPID about!

Six-time world middleweight martial arts champion, actor, and my very good friend Chuck Norris.

I say if people know that they are in danger of drowning and they go back into the Gulf when the red flag is flying, just send out the "STUPID Patrol" to retrieve the body when they wash ashore. Why do we want to risk our fine firemen, EMTs, and lifeguards to rescue STUPID people! I say let them be STUPID and let's "thin out the herd" and get on with life on the island! When we are interviewed by CNN about why so many people drown here, we can say, "Well; it was just stupid people; it's not like we lost our best and brightest, you know." It is the biggest example of mass stupidity I have ever seen.

I wonder if when you go to heaven, you have to have holes drilled in your back for the wings. I wonder if dogs and cats chase each other just to put on a show for us, cause they seem to get along fine as long as we are not looking at them. I wonder if babies know that they have a soft spot in their heads for the first six months and if they do, do they want to touch it? I know I would! I wonder if there is a confession booth for Catholic priests, and if there is, who do they confess to? It seems that they'd have to get a direct line to the Pope in Rome, to get high enough to find someone to confess to.

And finally, I wonder why I ponder so much. It seems that I never get any answers—not that I want any; I'm not sure what I would do with them!

Just thought you'd like to know...

If They Can Land a Man on the Moon...

Well, it's been many years since man landed on the moon. I remember it well. I stayed home from work to see President Nixon speak to Neil Armstrong by phone on the moon. It was exciting! Ever since then, I have heard the expression: "If they can land a man on the moon, why can't they..." and they would go on to ask "why" something! I have collected a few of the things "they" should be able to do!! We are slow sometimes as Americans. After all, we put a man on the moon before we thought that wheels on luggage would be a good idea!

So, if they can land a man on the moon, why can't they:

- Invent a TV remote control to find the regular one?

- Find the difference between indecent and obscene?

- Invent a road map that folds itself?

- Have dentists with small hands?

- Find a cure for Rosie O'Donnell?

- Find Elvis, Osama Bin Laden, and my real daddy?

- Invent big paper towels capable of cleaning up oil spills?

- Create TV newscasters who don't try to be funny?

- Explain why Pluto is not a planet anymore and just what a "dwarf" planet is?

- Make credit cards that show their limit with a flashing light? My entire wallet would be one big strobe light.

- Discover ethics in Congress? Or at least a way to implant it there.

- Invent drugs that make you smarter and better looking?

- Get Americans to land on Mars, so we can have a new saying, "If they can land a man on Mars, why can't they...?"

Just thought you'd like to know...

More Ponderings from Bubba's Beach

Last week I was pondering while sitting on my favorite island sand dune and watching birds at play on the beach. There wasn't another human in sight. It was one of those days that makes you feel good just to be alive. No humidity. The water was all five of my favorite colors and I was alone. The only unnatural thing I could see was my motorcycle parked on the side of the broken road.

I ponder a lot when I'm alone. As a matter of fact, it's very hard to do it any other way. I ponder:

- When the last condo is blown away...

- When the last scrub oak has died due to another subdivision or saltwater intrusion...

- When the last oil and gas well runs dry...

- When the last fish has been caught...

- When the last road that leads to nowhere sinks into the sand...

- When the last forest has been cleared...

- When the last stream has been poisoned...

- When the last sea turtle comes ashore to lay her eggs...

- When the last square foot of beautiful beach sand is covered with a four-lane road we never needed, condo footprints, bars, and asphalt...

- When the last green mountain turns brown...

- When the last brown wheat field turns to dust again...

- When the last farmer shuts down because he can't afford to follow his beloved profession...

- When the last president thinks we don't need to protect ourselves from the terrorists that want us all dead...

- When the last iceberg becomes just fresh water in a sea of salt...

- When the last immigrant comes to America looking for a "hand-out" and not a "way out"...

- When the last miner dies in a cave in what should never have happened...

- When the last union member drains the last dollar out of a corporation for his "entitlements"...

- When the last full moon can't be seen for the pollution...

- And when the last church closes because no one believes any longer... we will finally discover that we can't eat money.

Just thought you'd like to know...

CHAPTER 3

Fun on the Home Front

Someone once said, "Home is where the heart is." I don't believe that. To me, "home is where your memories are." When I'm with my children and Tarsha, on the other side of nowhere, I'm home! Home is where we go in our minds when we relive our lives. This chapter is the part of my book where I let you into my home. This is the "good stuff," the stuff that makes life worth living. It is a mixture spanning thirty years of love, life, and laughter.

Telemarketers Beware

Don't you just hate those folks who call to sell you something just as you sit down to eat, EVERY evening? I have found a way to prevent them from ever calling again, and sometimes even be removed from their list entirely! Use these and learn to enjoy their calls, even look forward to them! Let me show you what I mean.

Sometimes, when they ask if Mr. or Ms. Whatever is there, I say, "No, they both died. I inherited the house and the phone number. Do you want to come to the funeral? I've been getting calls all day from people, but not one casket seller. Do you know someone I could call for a cheap casket?" Most of them will just hang up at this point!

When they give me their name first, I will sometimes shout into the phone, "John, I thought that was you. Man, I ain't heard from you in a long time, how's-ya-mama-enem?" When he or she tries to explain that they don't know you, just don't believe it. Say, "I'd know your voice any- where..." or "I thought you got a job in politics selling manure." This will send them packing as well.

I also love to tell them I just got out on parole and I'm looking for a job. I say, "I learned about telemarketing in prison. I know all the laws and even ran a marketing scam from my cell. I made over $12,000 in three weeks before the warden found out. I'd be real good at it. Can I talk to your supervisor?" I have had a few actually put me on line with the super- visor. I tell the super I want to come down right now just as soon as I finish cleaning my gun. A clear hang-up often takes place here!

I love it when I get one that is a bit young; you can pick them out every time. I say, "I'm busy at this moment, but I'm interested. Can you give me your number and let me call you back in five minutes?" The phone number usually won't come over the caller ID. I have had a few of them actually give me their number. I call back and ask for them and when they come back on the phone, I say, "Hey, I got an old screen door and a female lop-eared bunny for sale, cheap. Do you have a credit card handy? I can get them right out to you." Often, a long pause follows and a dial tone!

Or I'll tell them, "My wife takes care of all the business in the family." Then I call my wife to the phone and tell her "Honey, it's for you!" You don't want to do this a lot, but the first two times can be very funny. 'Lishous threw the phone at me last time and would have hit me if I had not been rolling on the floor laughing.

Sometimes I'll say, "Yes, the man of the house is here," pause a few minutes, and then come back on the line as a person that stutters. I stutter

T. Bubba and "Lishous."

a lot, take five minutes to get a few words out, and then listen to their response. That one is a hoot!

I guess everybody has to make a living, but as long as you have a job that requires you to wear a nametag or pester people, you can expect the Bubbas of the world to bring a bit of joy into your life. I hope they can take it as well as dish it out. I know I can!

Just thought you'd like to know...

Too Much TV

My oldest son at six years old was seeing his first Passion Play. Performed by an out-of-town theater troupe at First Baptist Church in downtown Pensacola, the show was very graphic. As the Roman soldiers were nailing Jesus to the cross, the hammering rang out all over the church. It was a very dramatic moment; the large silent pause was almost too much to bear. We learned the hard way we had been letting him watch far too much television, when my son stood up in the church pew, pointed his finger at the stage, and yelled at the top of his lungs, "Don't worry, Jesus, Starski and Hutch will get those bad guys!"

Then the laughter erupted. The entire church of almost 2,000 people was bent over in uncontrollable hilarity. People had tears running down their cheeks. The actor on the cross was laughing so hard the fake blood was jumping off his body and the actors were hugging each other as they just lost it completely! Bubba Jr. knew he had added to the program and was smiling, and he even took a bow! His mother was horrified and snatched him up and ran out of the church. I followed and high-fived a few friends as I ran down the aisle. I was laughing so hard I sat down on the steps when I got outside the church.

At about that time, I saw my wife did not see any of the humor in this thing and was flaming angry red in the face and spitting her words at me. She asked, "What do you think is so funny? Don't you know he ruined the entire service, and you are letting him think that it is okay. He deserves a whipping, not your approval!" I knew right then I needed to sell my three businesses and become a comedian because I not only did not whip him, I took him for an ice cream cone and we laughed and ate ice cream while she sat and steamed in the car! She never did "get it!" And she never did "get me." About twenty years later she did "get" a divorce.

Just thought you'd like to know...

First Day

On my son's first day in school over thirty years ago, I sent the following note with him to his teacher. It has been printed in many newspapers and magazines around the world and is one of the best things I have ever written. It read;

Dear Teacher:

My son starts school today. It's going to be strange and new to him for a while. I wish you would sort of treat him gently. You see, up to now he's been king of the cul-de-sac. He's been boss of the backyard, prince of the pool and center of all attention.

I have always been there to repair his ego and soothe his temper. But now, things are going to be different. He's going to walk down the front steps, wave his hand and start on his great adventure that will probably include wars, tragedy and sorrow.

To live his life in this world he has to live in will require faith, forgiveness and courage. So, world, I wish you would take him by his small young hand and teach him the things he will have to know. Teach him, but gently, if you can.

Teach him that for every scoundrel, there is a hero; that for every crooked politician, there is a dedicated statesman; for every enemy, there is a friend.

Teach him the wonders of books and the joy of learning.

Teach him that for every scoundrel, there is a hero; that for every crooked politician, there is a dedicated statesman; for every enemy, there is a friend.

Give him quiet time to ponder the eternal mystery of birds in flight, sea oats at dawn, bees in the sun and flowers on a green hill.

Teach him that if he has to cheat to win, it is far more honorable to fail.

Teach him to have faith in his own ideas, even if all others tell him they are wrong.

Teach him to sell his brawn and brain to the highest bidder, but to never put a price on his heart and soul.

Teach him to say no to drugs, to close his ears to the howling mob and to stand and fight when he knows he is right, even if he is the only one standing.

Teach him gently, world, but don't coddle him, because only the test of fire can make fine steel, and thus far he has tempered well.

This is a big order I know, but see what you can do.

I will always be ready to teach him with you, should you call for help. I know that we are in this together, you and I.

I also know that you can't love him like I do, but teach him well. He's such a nice little fellow.

Dad

The Baseball Shakedown

I was at the local ballpark for a Pensacola Pelicans baseball game last night and was sitting next to a man that looked like he was new to the area. He had on one of those sleeveless shirts I use for undershirts, with Harley Logo boots on, and he talked sorta funny! I could tell he wasn't from around here. I asked him where he was from and he said, "Up Nawth!" I guess he wasn't born in a state, just an area. He didn't carry on the conversation, so I went back to watching the ball game.

The Pelicans were way ahead in a few innings, after two home runs and a grand slam. I went back to him and this time I asked him "What do you do?" He looked at me like I was from the IRS and said, "Why do you need to know?" I told him, "I don't *need* to know; I was just being friendly!" It was a strange concept to him. Why, talking to a total stranger asking such personal questions was unheard of to him!

I decided to have some fun. I was way larger than him, and he was alone. So I said, "I work for the Homeland Security Department and I followed you here to ask you a few questions!" His eyes got as big as the hubcaps on a monster truck. He looked me over for a minute and then said, "Well, sir I ain't no terrorist or nothing!"

I actually had him on the line, so I set the hook! I replied very seriously, even whispered to him, "Well, you look like a terrorist to me with all them tattoos and them thick-soled shoes you got on! You also were not very friendly, and it looked to me like you were scoping the stadium out for a bombing or something!"

"Well, you look like a terrorist to me with all them tattoos and them thick-soled shoes you got on!"

With this, he began to look around for some help or something. Everyone sitting around us was looking at him a bit strange by this time as well. He stood up and said, "Look mister, here's my driver's license and my ID card. I'm just down here doing sheetrock work for a family in Pace and came out to see the ballgame, I swear!" I knew I had taken it too far when his hand was trembling trying to get his license out of his wallet.

Just before I could smile and tell him who I really was, someone about two rows up from us yelled out, "Hey Bubba, tell that man next to you to sit down, and cut that crap out, you are scaring the hell out of him!" When the crowd around us began to laugh uncontrollably, the jig was up. Now, it was his turn and to my great fortune he began to smile and then began to laugh as loud as everyone else. It was a hoot!

But I got a glimpse of his driver's license before he took it back, and he was from Vermont. To think a big fat man, in a Pelican ballcap, cut-off blue jeans, and shower flipflops could be from Homeland Security anyway! Bless their hearts, they need to get out more!

Just thought you'd like to know...

Complaints for the Landlord

I recently did a show for an association of apartment managers and landlords.

The man that got up before me read out a list of complaints he has saved from renters for years. It was just a hoot. There was no need to have hired me; he was great. Here are a few excerpts that you will just love! He asked not to be identified and I can understand why!! Here they are:

- "I want some repairs done to my cooker as it has backfired and burnt my knob off."

- "I wish to complain that my father hurt his ankle very badly when he put his foot in the hole in his back passage."

- "My lavatory seat is cracked; where do I stand?"

- "Will you please send someone to mend the garden path? My wife tripped and fell on it yesterday and now she is pregnant."

- "I request permission to remove my drawers in the kitchen."

- "I am still having problems with smoke in my new drawers."

- "The toilet is blocked and we cannot bathe the children until it is cleared."

- "Would you please send a man to repair my spout? I am an old-age pensioner and use it often."

- "The man next door has a large erection in the back garden, which is unsightly and dangerous."

- "I am a single woman living in a downstairs flat, and would you please do something about the noise made by the man I have on top of me every night? He's got this huge tool that vibrates the whole house and I just can't take it anymore."

- "It's his excuse for the dog's mess that I find hard to swallow."

- "This is to inform you that my toilet seat is broken and I can't get channel 9."

Now ain't you glad you ain't a landlord?

Just thought you'd like to know...

Haircuts

I don't know why getting a haircut has gotten so hard to do.

Things used to be simple. I went to Harry or Eddie, they gave me a cut and trim, shaved my neck, dusted me with talcum powder, slapped on some toilet water, and I paid them and left happy. I looked good, was

T. Bubba on the set of a video shoot for country music parody star Cletus T. Judd.
T. Bubba did four with Cletus.

socially acceptable, and I went twice a month. It was a fun time as well. There were men's magazines to look through, the latest sports were discussed, and even when they hired a lady barber, she became one of the guys real soon!

Nowadays, you go to "The Hairy Place" or "The Happy Shears" and two women with pierced eyelids and green lipstick greet you with options! You can get shampooed, cut, and blow-dried for $102, and that don't include the tip. You can get a razor cut, a slide cut, or an ear cut for under

$90, but when you are through you look like you have more hair than you came in with. You will get a chair next to some woman that is having her hair dyed blue for her husband's 81st birthday and can't stop talking about "how much she hates it here!"

The chairs are too small, the mirrors are cluttered with photos of the cutters' kids in Halloween, birthday, and class poses, and it becomes apparent this woman should not be allowed to procreate ever again!

The "barber shop" has almost disappeared and with it the last vestige of manly haircuts. None of these women today know how to level a flattop, cut a mullet, or mold the remaining hair a man may have to his bald skull to make him more handsome—not one! I have to go to a salon and beg for "just a trim." After I show her how to do it, it costs me $35 and I get to tip Dracula for a haircut my brother could have given me with a bowl and his pocket knife!

Bless their hearts...

Just thought you'd like to know...

Feeling the Heat

Well, it is summertime again. I moved to Florida because I liked the sun, but I didn't sign on for the humidity. It is HOT! The heat index was too high to report today; the weatherman didn't want to kill anyone with the announcement.

It's so hot I got hot water coming out of both taps. I saw some shade way out in the parking lot and parked there because walking a mile to the store was better than dying when I got back into my car. It was still hot when I got back there, though. I tried to buckle my seatbelt and that thing was so hot, it scarred me for life. Now I have a permanent brand in the palm of my hand that says "Jeep." When I shake hands with someone, they feel the "Jeep" and wonder what type of pervert I really am. I keep eight fingers in my mouth now when I'm driving and alternate the use of two at a time on the steering wheel!

I like sun-steeped tea. I put a jar out yesterday and it was done in ninety seconds. I broke into a sweat in my shower today! I went for a bike ride and was worried I would fall down and fry to death on the sidewalk before I could get back up! My driveway melted!

I saw a cat explode yesterday from the heat. It just blew up right there in front of me. Its eyes bulged, the hair stood on end, and it just exploded! I saw a dog chasing a cat and they were both walking. It's HOT!

I understand the local farmers are feeding their chickens ice to keep them from laying boiled eggs! I heard a tree whistle for a dog yesterday. I don't know when it will end, but since the cold spell we had for the last three weeks left, I think Mother Nature is making up for it.

Knock if you come to my house because I have stopped wearing any clothes. I only wear a bathing suit when I go outside and an ice bag on each foot. It looks weird, but I'm walking, ain't I? It's HOT, in case you haven't noticed.

Just thought you'd like to know...

You Know You're in South Florida When...

Florida is the only state in Dixie that is upside down. The further south you go, the more north you get; and when you get to Ft. Lauderdale and Miami, you are back in New York and New Jersey.

The true southern part of Florida is located in the northern part of the state. The "Mason Dixon line" is Ocala. You can't get good Bar-B-Q south of Ocala, and from there northward and west to the Alabama line, you will find the gracious art of southern living still survives. It survives best between Tallahassee and Pensacola, the pure "southern" part of the state. The "real south" is located in the real northern and western part of the state. Doncha just love it?

Long Island in New York used to be called "Longer Island;" a big piece of it broke off years ago and floated south and reattached itself right around Ft. Lauderdale. South Florida is the land of newlyweds and nearly deads. The average age there is "deceased," and the only thing to ever come out of south Florida that was worth two spits is Interstate 95 North.

So, here are a few ways you can tell you are in south Florida, other than the foreign language and the smell.

- Your girlfriend has two body piercings, but won't show you where!

- You are shocked at two people carrying on a conversation in English.

- Your child's third-grade teacher has blue hair, a nose ring, and a degree from Berkeley and is named Wind Dancer.

- You can't remember... how old is old?

- You've been to a Rosie O'Donald baby shower that had two mothers and a sperm donor.

- You have a very strong opinion about where your coffee beans are grown and can taste the difference between Columbian and Cuban.

- A really great parking space can move you to tears, and the interstate is two feet six inches from your bedroom window.

- Your car insurance costs as much as your house payment.

- Your hairdresser is straight, your plumber is gay, the woman who delivers your mail is into S&M, and your Mary Kay rep is a guy in drag that looks like someone just sprayed him with Pepto-Bismol pink.

- It's sprinkling out and there's a report on every news station about the upcoming hurricane season.

Your hairdresser is straight, your plumber is gay,
the woman who delivers your mail is into S&M...

- It's sprinkling outside, so you leave for work an hour early to avoid all the weather-related accidents.

- Fidel Castro's picture is on every telephone post in a six-mile area.

- A conservative republican is a Cuban, is straight, and actually has a job.

- You know that North Florida exists, but have no idea where it is.

- You are a Miami Hurricanes fan at a white school, with a black football team, in a city of brown people that don't speak English.

God, I love southern Florida up here in the northwest Florida Panhandle, of course.

Just thought you'd like to know...

Things That Don't Go Together

My neighbor and fellow Bubbette, Alice, and I were talking one day and we decided that there are fads nowadays that just don't go together. I see some weird-looking people out there, and I'm not talking about just the young people. To me, nothing is sadder than an old hippy, hanging on to the past. Bald and hair weaves just do not go together, and paisley and size 58 don't either. With that in mind, here are a few things that we see today that "just don't go together:"

- A nose ring and bifocals are a NO-NO! It just makes the nose look even smaller and the ring loses its appeal.

- Spiked hair and bald spots look like a disease or the mange.

- If you have dentures, leave out the pierced tongue; the clicking sound just drives me nuts!

- Mini-skirts and support hose make you look like a stork that ate way too much, and if you have a corn pad on, leave the ankle bracelet at home.

- When at the beach, leave the French-cut bathing suit in the bag if you have cellulite from your knees to your butt. Why don't best friends tell each other about cellulite? If they would, the world would be much more beautiful.

- If you have had a tummy tuck, please don't insist on the belly button ring. It just draws the eye to the scar, and we don't want to know why it's there! I saw an old man with his shirt unbuttoned to the waist last week that had heart surgery scars that made him look like a road map of Arizona!

A nose ring and bifocals are a NO-NO!
It just makes the nose look even smaller and
the ring loses its appeal.

- If you have midriff bulge, wear a shirt; and if you have to shave your back, get acquainted with long-sleeved T shirts, without logos or funny quotes on them. I saw a fat lady last week wearing a sweatshirt that said "GUESS" on the front of it. I said, "Okay, about 320 pounds!" She hit me with her bag of bagels and called the police on me! If you don't want an answer, don't advertise!

- If you have liver spots, hang up the bikini! If you have a body like the Michelin Tire man, cover up totally and understand that your bathing suit days are over!

- If kids keep throwing water on you while you are lying on the beach, yelling, "keep it moist until we get it back into the water, or it will sunburn," go on a diet!

- And oh yeah, don't wear bathing suits and short shorts if you have varicose veins. Don't even wear pedal pushers; we don't want even a glimpse! If your underarms flap in the wind, give away the tank tops and buy nothing without long sleeves until you die.

It's up to you, America, to "cover up" when you can't "glamour up" anymore! Keep your ugly secrets to yourself. Tell your best friend to let you know when you need to buy a one-piece bathing suit and it's time to stop wearing shorts totally. Don't be like old athletes that don't know when the game is over. Know when the sag is in the bag, don't make us all gag! Man, I'm starting to sound like Jesse Jackson now! But, ladies, when you got too much "junk in the trunk," stop trying to haul it around without a tarp over it! I'm twice the size I was in my younger days, and I'm enjoying every inch and pound of it, but I don't want to share it with you or the inspecting tourist that comes here from Utah! I want them to come back. I like it when they spend money; it keeps the tax man away a bit longer! Just remember, when you can't anymore SHOW IT, then STOW IT! Please!!

Just thought you'd like to know...

Bras of Hope

A radio station in Mobile, Alabama, just did a promotion on National Breast Cancer Month. They collected over 5,000 brassieres and hung them in Colonial Belle Air Mall from a "Tree of Hope."

What?!!

Am I the only one who thinks this is bizarre? I say that we not follow this promotion. Can you imagine 5,000 pair of men's underwear hanging from the "Tree of Prostate" to promote Testicular Month? NOOOO! Enough is enough; I say "Let's not go there!" I don't want to see thousands of jockey straps hanging from anything to promote anything, okay? Why, the islanders here would have this not suitable for viewing in no time! They would take this little promotion and turn it into something that adults, much less children, should never have to look upon! Can you imagine what would happen if the island Mardi Gras krewes got hold of this? Why, we'd have Mardi Gras floats made completely of men's and women's underwear. They would be throwing out beads tangled with bras at the next parade, and that ain't cool! And I sure don't want to catch a nice set of beads attached to an old pair of grandpa's boxers.

I'm all for raising money for and supporting National Breast Cancer Month, but I'm not going to travel to see a Tree of Hope filled with bras of all sizes and shapes... and who knows what they smell like? You know what they should have done with those bras? I say they should have cut them in half and added strips of cloth from one side of the cup to the other, and then they would have had 10,000 beanies with chin straps! Now that would be a promotion worth going to and supporting. The Bubbas of the world could add a little propeller to the top and have the coolest beanies in the world. It's just a thought!

Just thought you'd like to know...

CHAPTER 4

Bubba Wisdom from the Heart

A True Leader

A "Bubba" doesn't see the world the way the rest of the "normal" people do. His wisdom is based on exactly how he views the world. Bubba is not afraid to say what is on his mind... just like young children and old folks do. Bubba is both of these, just in an older body... a true leader. I spent years in the nation's number one leadership training organization for young people: the United States Jaycees (or the Junior Chamber of Commerce to some of the older folks). I went from local president of the Escambia Bay Jaycees to Florida president, and in 1980 served as national president. I went from there directly to the "Reagan for President" (RNC) campaign. I served several years with the RNC before coming home to run my first race for U.S. congressman from this district in 1982.

While with the RNC, I had the opportunity to be around one of the twentieth-century's greatest leaders. Ronald Reagan led with courage, convictions, goals, and some even say with some old movie lines. Many say he was nothing but a cheerleader. But if he was, our nation really needed a cheerleader when he came along.

I was serving as chairman of the board of the U.S. Jaycees and was on a trip in Alabama in the early 80s. I was invited by some of my GOP friends to attend an event with Ronald Reagan. There were a lot of important people traveling with him: senators, ambassadors, and his staff—the entire White House group. It was then that I saw him at one of his greatest moments. This true leader took a potentially embarrassing and discouraging situation and found a way to keep things upbeat. We were in Alabama at a special school for handicapped children that the Jaycees had raised a lot of money for and had supported with community projects. I felt that it

T. Bubba at the White House with President Ronald Reagan, a true leader.

was a "photo op" and was not really into it until he rose to speak. He offered a few minutes of remarks and took questions from the kids. It was unreal. The president of the United States was talking with and answering questions from children who had no idea who he was. All they knew was that he was kind, was fun, and wanted to talk with them. Only later would they realize the importance of this meeting. It would likely have a great impact on them for years to come.

He answered every question they had. One asked if he had his own airplane. He said, "No, it belongs to the people of the United States, but they let me ride in it when I want to." The kid said, "Well can we take a trip in it now?" The room roared. One child then said, "Haven't I seen you on TV?" They were handicapped children, he was the president, and I was spellbound at how he was reacting to this special event.

Then one child stood up. When he began to speak, the room went totally silent. This child had a severe speech impediment. He asked his question and no one in the room could understand it. The president asked him if he could repeat it and again no one could understand what was said. The room froze. My eyes went to the TV cameras and they were pointing to the floor. The teacher was by the kid's side, not knowing what to do. None of us knew what to do. What was to have been an upbeat day for everyone was turning into a disaster. Instead of allowing the wonderful kids to forget about their handicap, this moment was going to remind them all of their limitations. Reagan, the leader, however, knew what to do. It came naturally, without effort, with compassion, and right on time.

The most powerful man in the Free World, the president of our country, leaned toward the child and he smiled that famous smile, chuckled, and said, "Well, I'm sorry, but you know I've got this hearing aid in my ear. Every once in a while the darn thing just conks out on me. And it's just gone dead. Sorry to put you through this again, but I'm going to ask one of my staff people to go over to you so you can tell him directly what your question is. Then he can pass the question back to me. Would that be okay?" Rather than embarrass the child in front of his class, Reagan brought up his own handicap.

Is it any wonder that he was loved by millions, regardless of their politics? Now that's leadership. God give us more like him.

Just thought you'd like to know...

I Don't Know How We Survived

When I look back over my life, I don't know how I lived to grow to the age I am now. We did everything the experts today say will kill you. How could we possibly have more people in this country over fifty years of age than under fifty? I don't know how we did the things we did and are still the majority of the population.

We rode in cars without seatbelts, we rode in the back of pick-up trucks, and we ate whatever we wanted without regard to fat content. We painted cribs with varnish, wood stain, lead-based paint; and for the most part we cut our teeth on the crib, swallowed the stuff, and laughed about it. There was nothing "childproof." We could open a medicine bottle and cabinet doors at four years old, and I never saw a bike helmet until I was almost thirty years old. I thought they looked stupid then and I do now. We drank water from streams and ponds and I once drank from a stump hole and had to move the green scum aside to get to it. I never had so much as a stomachache!

As a matter of fact, I think maybe that caused me never to have bad gas to this very day! We built "go carts" out of creosote railroad ties, put asbestos tiles on them for traction, and ran them down a hill into traffic hundreds of times. The only problem we ever had was once when Buster Bilbo fell off and put a knot on his head the size of a softball. Buster was better off for it, because he began to talk real words. Until then he had only been able to make the sound of a log truck changing gears! We solved the brakes problem by dragging our bare feet on the ground, and today I can walk barefoot over glass and never feel it.

My mother never knew where we were, but she didn't worry about us either. She knew if we were not home by sundown we were in trouble.

Either way we got whipped with a peach branch around our legs, and if we cried we got stripped and got a real butt-whuppin'! We were always home by sundown.

We jumped out of trees, swam in a swamp, killed snakes on sight. When we were old enough to play Little League, only the best players made it and the ones that didn't make the team had to deal with the disappointment. It made them try harder the next year and taught them determination and how to be better people.

"Son, if you don't make anything other than C's on your report card, you are just average, and average is the 'cream of the crap.'"

Some students were smarter than others, and those that didn't make the grade were failed and held back until they got smarter. It made "positive peer pressure" a thing to behold! We made more kids graduate on time by making fun of them. A much more effective method than the "advanced teaching aids" of today will ever be! We smoked until we figured out it was stupid and stopped on our own without blaming the tobacco companies. We drank until we learned if we wanted to "make it" we had to act different in public. Drunks were drunks even then, and we knew we had to grow up or remain stuck in the muck we were in at the time. It was motivation enough!

We had "no pass, no play" in my high school athletic programs forty years ago—but my momma enforced it, NOT the government! I look back and laugh at today's politically correct world and wonder just what we are doing to our children.

We had the freedom to be stupid. We learned that to "fail" was not socially correct and was a dead-end street as well. We wanted success because we knew "it was expected of us." We learned responsibility, work ethics, and how to deal with life on our own. We knew if we didn't succeed, we would be considered a failure. In my world, I was more afraid of being a failure than I was of failing, so I worked hard not to fail. The rest took care of itself! Today children learn everybody is somebody regardless of their station in life and it has led us to the desire to be average.

Finally, I'll never forget my grandfather's definition of average. He told me one day, "Son, if you don't make anything other than C's on your report card, you are just average, and average is the 'cream of the crap.'" I never wanted to be the best of the worst since that very conversation. I wonder if we can teach that to our children today.

Just thought you'd like to know...

Life and Reasons

Life is reason. Long life is reasons. There is a reason for everything in life and when you take control of the reasons, you gain control of the results.

If you want respect in this life, give people a good hard reason to respect you. Even an animal will not respect you if you don't earn it.

I was a very young man when I learned that reasons are the way to respect. My mother told me once, "Son, if you do more than is expected of you, you will be respected. When you are respected, you will then have choices, and choices are what life is all about!"

Wise woman, my mother. I always tried to do more than was expected of me. I made a lot of mistakes, I hurt some people on the way, and I have a few things that I wish to hell I could go back and make right. I am still a work in progress. But life moves on, and so do reasons for living it.

Money is earned for a reason. People fall in love for a reason. Businesses rise and fall for reasons, and if you are successful in life there is a reason for it. A great reason is created; it doesn't just happen. You have to make a reason.

I wanted to learn to play golf. I was a great athlete in my younger life; I knew I could do it, but doing it well has been a thirty-eight-year obsession. It is the hardest thing I ever tried to do in sports, bar none. I see people taking up the game and discovering for the first time that they I can't do something. It is hard, it will humble you; it is a great game that not many people play very well.

What was the reason I kept playing a game I sucked at? The reason is simple: It challenged me more than anything in my life, and it still does. I may die never having broken 90, but I have created a love for the game and that is the reason I still play it. The people that give it up just don't have a good enough reason to continue.

I married the woman I married for a reason. I had been single for eighteen years; life was good, lots of ladies, good friends, and fun. I was alone, but I was not lonely! Then this woman came into my life that gave me a reason to have two cats in my home. The cats are messy, have no reason to live, and don't care about anything but themselves. But the reason they are living is a $20,000 addition I made to my home, that I no longer go into, because one day I sat down and realized I was in love. The kind of love that makes you stupid. That wonderful kind of love that takes you a lifetime to get used to.

The reason the cats became unimportant and I decided that I could live with this woman was this: You don't marry someone you can live with; you marry someone that you can't live without. So far it has been a good reason. I love you Lishous.

Once you have a reason, you have created a cause and the effect will determine how good a reason you have. If you give life good reasons for success, love, and respect to come your way, it will. I know it has for me.

Just thought you'd like to know...

May Day Birthday

I have a birthday coming up on May 1. Yes, I was born on "May Day." It also is the international distress signal, "May Day, May Day!!" It is not just happenstance that this is exactly what my mother was screaming aloud

"Big Baby" T. Bubba at three months old.

during my entire birth process. I was a large baby. So large that I never fully grew into myself, it seems. (I'm not sure what that means, but it reads so well.) I was 16.4 pounds... now that's a big baby. I was actually born on May 1st, 2nd, and 3rd! When the doctor slapped me, I slapped him back! They had to stand on a ladder to take my baby picture!

What have I learned in these so many years? As my knowledge grows into wisdom and my chest continues to fall into my drawers, just what do I have to pass on to the two generations behind me? First, let me say that these are not recommendations, just things that I have learned. You will have to learn your own things to pass on.

- Life is like toilet paper; the closer to the end you get, the faster it goes. I don't know who said this first but he was a Bubba for sure.

- It is the little things in life that make it worth living, not the big things that shape a life.

- To ignore the facts does not ever change the facts, just the attitude about the facts.

- My wife is my best friend, and I pity the man that can't say the same.

- My dog is the only thing in the world that loves me unconditionally.

- Time does not heal wounds; only love can do this. Time just makes us numb to the pain. Words and actions heal wounds... never time.

- If you can't forget, then you can never forgive. Forgiving is forgetting and never using what you forgave against the forgiven.

- No woman is perfect until you fall in love with her.

- The sweetest memory in my life is holding my sons while they slept and feeling their breath against my cheek. Second is watching them fall asleep as I sang "Danny Boy" to them!

- Opportunities are never lost. Someone will use the ones you miss. Count on it.

- I cannot choose how I feel, but I can do something about the way others feel about me.

- When you are filled with bitterness, happiness will find another place to live.

- Smiles can be felt through a telephone; grins are just smiles that broke wide open.

- And finally, my life IS my life's work, and when it is over it will be judged by other people. That is why I have never said, "I don't care what other people think about me; it's my life and I'm going to live it the way I want to!" What other people think about you IS your life, whether you like it or not. Nuff said!

Just thought you'd like to know...

Life to Bubba

I have lived longer than I thought I would. When I was young, I had grand ideas of dying young and leaving a bright star for all to remember. I thought I was a comet streaking through the sky brilliantly and then gone in a flash.

I know now that was the foolishness of youthful thinking. I did not die young, and if I had died young, I would have left no mark on life at all.

Life began to happen and I found myself in the midst of excitement. The things that were happening to me were things that only happened to people in the movies. I met presidents, met two kings, became a leader in my community, entered politics, and began to travel the world. I want to give back what I have learned, but it's hard to find anyone who wants it. Now that I'm a "seasoned citizen," as I look back over my life I realize that I'm just an old star, full of gas that is beginning to fade.

I have shaken my fists at congressmen, senators, preachers, IGMOs, bad drivers, ugly women, unpatriotic un-American people, bad teachers, and one ex-wife. It's time now to open my hands to the world.

When was the last time you asked yourself, "Is my brightest and best over?" Mine is not. I know now that "a closed mouth gathers no foot." Last week in a local department store, I told a young man that would not give me a chance to explain what I wanted in return for my money, "Son, it's hard to ever learn anything when your mouth is moving!" He got it and, to his credit, shut up and let me tell him what I wanted. I look at my friends and wonder why I ever thought they were normal. I have strange friends, but they all fit me to a T. Then there are false friends. Like people I loaned money to that never paid me back and never associated with me anymore. It was worth the money.

I never jump into the water head first any longer, and when I test deep water I only use one foot. I am going to enjoy this "senior" phase of my life. I don't know how to stop working. How do you retire from making people laugh? I know I'll never see one dime of my social security, but that is all right. I'd just like to know that it is going to go to someone that really needs the help. I don't need help. I need more friends, more time to enjoy them, and for my wife to stay home more and sit with me and watch the sunsets. I'm a lucky man. I have sons that I can brag about and a dog that will bite anyone who threatens me. My sugar is up, my blood pressure is too, and I can't make a fist any longer because of my arthritis. However, I don't need to make fists anymore. I have shaken my fists at congressmen, senators, preachers, IGMOs, bad drivers, ugly women, unpatriotic un-American people, bad teachers, and one ex-wife. It's time now to open my hands to the world.

What I need now is to laugh more, love more, and get ready to be that crotchety old man that is never wrong, says what is on his mind, and makes you wonder if he is going to cuss you or hit you. Yep, that is the ticket. I can't wait. I have earned it, and I'm going to love it.

Just thought you d like to know...

The Value of Time

My wife told me yesterday that she "would be home sometime." I don't know when that is. I don't know if time is some or many. I'm not even sure what time really is. It has to be more than hands on a clock. It has to be the thing that we don't need to waste the least of. Time is an unsure thing to me.

Now that I'm older, it seems more important, but is it really? The time I spent with my sons, those people who touched me, and the ones that I touched along the way seems to have been time that I remember well now. All the time I wasted being less than I could be seems to have faded from my mind. I think that sitting in my island home watching a sunset that would make a trucker cry is a wonderful waste of time. So, what is the value of time?

- To realize the value of time spent with a father; ask someone who never had one.

- To realize the value of twenty years; ask an eighty-year-old person.

- To realize the value of one year, ask a student who has failed a final exam.

- To realize the value of one month, ask a mother who has given birth to a premature baby.

- To realize the value of one week, ask an editor of a weekly newspaper.

- To realize how long five seconds can be, hold your hand over an open flame.

- To realize the value of one minute, ask the person who has just missed his/her airplane.

- To realize the value of one millisecond, ask the person who wished they could take back harsh words just uttered.

Time is a man-made concept. Only humans even give a flip about it. Animals could care less. We say that time waits for no man, but women have never heard that statement. However, you should treasure every moment you have. The only way to make time worthwhile is to spend it with someone you love; anything else is time wasted. Life goes quickly; you only have one shot, but if you live it right, once is enough. Trust Ole Bubba on this one.

Just thought you'd like to know...

Momma's Advice

When I was a young man, one of the first of almost thirty grandchildren to ever graduate from high school and was on my way to a small college in southern Mississippi, my mother took me to the Trailways bus stop in Ocean Springs, Mississippi.

She was a hard woman who was raising four boys by herself on a garment worker's salary. She was very proud of her oldest son going off to

T. Bubba performing at the Grand Ole Opry.

college, but this U.S. Marine did not know how to say the words. I knew she loved me, even though she never told me until I was about to be married six years later. It was an awkward moment. I was headed for a big adventure that would take me to over fifty-six countries, become president of the United States Jaycees, become a candidate for the U.S. Congress, and end up as a comedian on the Grand Ole Opry stage. I didn't know what to say either. Everything I owned was in a brown A&P grocery bag and I had $6 in my pocket. I just looked at her and she looked at me.

Then she said these words to me. I did not understand them at the time, but came to know the meaning of them only after I saw my own sons go out into the world. I listened as she said, "Son, when you get to that college, almost every student there will have more than you. They will have nicer clothes, they will have more money, and they will know each other. When times get hard and you feel alone and not part of the group, just remember this. You come from good stock! Your ancestors didn't come over on the *Mayflower,* but they were the people who kept them from starving to death. Your grandfather is one of the most respected men of God in this part of the state, and you are there because you played football good enough for them to come and ask you to be there. The rest of them are paying for it! Just remember where you come from and try to make a path for your brothers to follow you." I said nothing, I did not know how to react, but I never forgot those words.

As the bus pulled up and people began to mill around, she looked at me with the faintest little mist in her eyes and said, "Son, whatever you do, live your life." Then she shoved a small folded piece of notebook paper into my hands and walked away. I thought it was the dumbest thing I had ever heard anyone say. I almost laughed. I was thinking, "Of course I'm gonna live my life; who else can?" I didn't get that one either.

As I watched her walk away, there were no hugs, no kisses, nothing but pride in her stride as I got on the bus. As we were crossing Biloxi Bay, I pulled out the note and read it. It said, "There was a very cautious man who never laughed or played. He never risked, he never tried, he never sang or prayed. And when he one day passed away, his insurance was denied. For since he never really lived, they claimed he never died."

I have tried to live up to spirit of that moment, and regardless of how many mistakes I have made in my life, whoever I have wronged or made laugh, for all the good or bad I have ever done, by God I have LIVED my life thus far. Have you?

Just thought you'd like to know...

The Tupperware Party

One evening after dinner, when 'Lil Bubba was about six years old, he noticed that his mother had gone out and he asked, "Where did mommy go?"

In answer to his questions, I told him, "Mommy is at a Tupperware party." This explanation satisfied him for only a moment.

Puzzled, he asked, "What's a Tupperware party, Dad?" I've always given my son honest answers, so I figured a simple explanation would be the best approach.

"Well, son," I said, "at a Tupperware party, a bunch of women sit around and sell plastic bowls to each other."

He nodded, indicating he understood this curious pastime. Then he burst into laughter. He was laughing so hard and then he said, "Come on, Dad, what is it really?"

It was a moment I will never forget; we laughed for an hour and had to go outside to stretch when it was over!

Just thought you'd like to know...

T. Bubba's son, Robert "Lil' Bubba" Bechtol growing up.

The Snoring Bubba

I was on a flight recently coming home from a show on the "left coast." I was tired, it was the last flight out of Atlanta, and the airplane was jammed full. I had the bad fortune to be seated beside a lady who was almost as large as I was, and we were both leaning to the right and left just so we could fit in our seats. I was on the aisle seat across from a wife and husband that had been flying all day and they looked much more haggard than I felt.

Just as soon as the plane took off, he was asleep. We could all hear him. He was in one of those sleeps that only a Bubba can love. He was a bit on "the Bubba side" with his weight, his hair had long since withdrawn, and he was perched in the middle seat between two women who wished they were seated someplace else. His wife had the aisle seat, and I never saw the woman in the window seat; she was totally blocked from view!

Ten minutes into the flight, the wife dug an elbow into his sides, told him to "Wake up, fool; you're disturbing everyone on the airplane!" He sat up, but to no avail. In two minutes he was snoring again. She shook him again to wake him up and this time got into his ear with words I cannot mention here. He sat up, tried to read the flight magazine, but nodded off into that far-away place that only he knows and was making snore sounds that drowned out the airplane engines. The flight attendants came around with peanuts and drinks, but his wife could not wake him up this time. She apologized to the attendants and told them, "If anyone complains, you'll have to deal with him yourself. I've had it with him; he is so embarrassing!" She said it so everyone in ten rows could hear her disassociate herself from the snoring Bubba.

About a minute after she made her statement, a little lady in the seat right behind me leaned over and touched her on the right arm to get her attention. When the woman turned around the lady said, "You know, I was married to the most wonderful man for fifty-one years. I lost him seven weeks and three days ago. I'd give every dime I own today, and live in poverty for the rest of my life, if I could just hear him snoring next to me in our bed just one more night." No one said a thing; no one needed to. We all just settled into our seats a bit and thanked our blessings for the little annoyances in our lives that remind us of love. I had to stop working my crossword puzzle. There was something in my eyes and I couldn't see the damn thing anymore.

Just thought you'd like to know...

Raising a "Good Girl"

God blessed me with two sons. I never raised a good girl, but I was married to one for twenty years. Once I asked her mother, "How did you raise such a good girl?" and she replied, "Son, when your child is out at 4:00 a.m. and you don't know where they are—when it is your son you

T. Bubba backstage with multi-platinum recording artist Jo Dee Messina.

worry, but when it is your daughter you pray." I never forgot it! I think boys are easier to raise than girls, especially when they begin to date.

I have a friend who is a fellow Bubba who has two daughters. In fact, Buster is the HBIC (Head Bubba in Charge) of all the Bubbas in the state of Texas. He has devised a set of rules that cover dating his daughters. I thought I'd pass them along to those of you who have girls who are of dating age:

- If you honk your horn when you drive up in my yard, you better be driving a big brown truck with UPS on the side, because otherwise you are sure not going to be picking up anything!

- Do not touch my daughter in front of me. Don't look, touch, or glance at anything below her neck. If you cannot keep your hands off my daughter, I will remove them for you.

- Do not show up in pants that look like they may fall off with your underwear showing. If you do, I will use my nailgun to attach them to your waistline where they belong. If you do not have a buckle on your belt, I have one that is big enough for you to use in a fight if you need to, or you can eat dinner for two off it. You will not leave my house with my daughter if your pants look like they may come off, because if they do, you need to have your next of kin tattooed on your behind!

- I understand in today's world, "sex without a barrier method" can kill you. Understand this: I am the barrier. If you have sex with her, I will kill you!

- Unless you date my daughter at her consent at least five times, I don't want to talk to you about football, baseball, politics, or any small talk. All I want to hear from you is when you will bring her home safe and all I want to hear on that subject is two words—one is "early" and the other is "sir."

- Upon the first date with my little girl, you will not date anyone else unless she is aware of it and consents to it. If you tell her, "I'll call you later" and you don't call her, I will call you. If you make her cry, I will make you cry. I will hurt you. Your momma and your entire family will never recognize you again!

- Do not take my daughter to places where refined young ladies should not be seen. Her momma and I spent thousands of dollars on her upbringing, and if you take her someplace like that and she ever calls me to come and get her, I will blow your house up and shoot your dog.

- Do not lie to me. I may appear to be a potbellied, balding, middle-aged, dimwitted Bubba. But on issues relating to my daughters, I am the all-knowing, merciless God of your universe. If I ask you where you are going and with whom, you have one chance to tell me the truth, the whole truth, and nothing but the truth. I have a shotgun, a shovel, and five acres behind the house. Do not mess with me.

- Be afraid. Be very afraid. It takes very little for me to mistake the sound of your car in the driveway for a chopper coming in over a rice paddy. The voices in my head frequently tell me to clean the guns as I wait for you to bring my daughter home. As soon as you pull into the driveway, you should exit your car with both hands in plain sight. Speak the perimeter password, announce in a clear voice that you have brought my daughter home safely and early, then return to your car. There is no need for you to come inside.

- If you ever refer to her with any disrespectful words or call her your "stuff," you will find it hard to speak without your tongue in the future. She is a lady. I did the best I could and when I give her over to another man in this lifetime, he will have earned the right to be hers and I will accept nothing less. If you do not feel you can aspire to these rules of the first date, don't let the door hit you on your way out!

Signed, Buster Bilbo, Father
Just thought you'd like to know...

Goodbye Lewis, We'll Miss You...

One day many years ago, I received a phone call from Atlanta to inquire if I could make a show date in Orlando to a group of heart surgeons to cover for the great Lewis Grizzard—popular columnist, best-selling author, and one great Bubba. Lewis had heart problems and could not make it. I covered for him and thus began a great chapter in my life.

Steven Lee Enoch, Lewis's personal manager for several years, became my manager after that date as we began to fill several other dates that Lewis could not get to. I became the pinch hitter for Lewis Grizzard Enterprises. I moved to Atlanta, and Steve and I began to work together to fill other show dates where southern humor was called for. Little did I know that Lewis was about to leave us. Lewis went in for his third heart surgery and died on the operating table at age forty-two—much too soon.

Lewis Grizzard was laid to rest on a beautiful spring day, next to his mother. It was all it should have been. A small southern town that came out to honor one of its own who had gone further and higher than anyone ever thought he would. A simple man who touched the world with his writings and humor. A man who was born thirty years too late, and his readers loved him for it. He never quite understood it when "Willie Nelson started wearing an earring" and people began to "eat mushrooms on their cheeseburgers." He was able to touch us all with the things we see in our lives and remind us that we are special just for being southern.

It was a simple service. People came out to tell stories about "them and Lewis" and to say goodbye. His favorite football coach, Ray Golf of the University of Georgia, his alma mater, set the tone when he began his eulogy with, "What can you say about Lewis Grizzard that you can say in a church?"

I believe that everyone lives as long as they are supposed to.

The beautiful widow wore appropriate red and his stepdaughter Jordan had placed a small troll doll in the casket with him. He was laid out at the wake in a Georgia red sports coat, plain white shirt, and, of course, no tie. While no one could see, I am sure that he had no socks on either; he never did! Proper and fitting again!

A group of his golfing buddies played a round of golf in his honor in the "missing man" formation. One said that "it was what Lewis would have done if it had been one of us, and the nearest I can figure out, he owes us each $11.50." Proper and fitting again.

After his untimely death, I never saw the South sadder. I loved the man. He was the most "southern" of all of us Southern Boys. Lewis was the original Smart-Ass Southern White Boy. He and I were each married for the first time on the same day, not too far apart. We grew up in the same type of small southern town, ate the same foods, loved the same football teams; and both of us grew up to travel the nation telling others about our southern outlooks on American life—he as a writer, me as a humorist. His best-selling books, cassette tapes, and personal appearances recalled a kinder, gentler South that we both longed for again. The "New South" we loved too, but we had never quite gotten the hang of it yet.

I feel blessed because I got to know a different Lewis than most of his childhood friends, his three ex-wives, and those that knew the biting satire that made him famous.

I got to know a Lewis that had come to believe in the power of prayer. A man that had come full circle and could respond to people that came up to him after both of his earlier heart surgeries and told him how they prayed for him during those tough times. His final year was filled with the love of a good woman and her daughter. He knew the love of a child before he left us. He married Dedra Kyle just four days before he died. For us he left a lifetime of humor, memories, and an example of how to get the most out of your life, regardless of circumstances.

I believe that everyone lives as long as they are supposed to. The length of a life has nothing whatsoever to do with the quality of it. We did not lose Lewis. We will always have him in the way we have Mark Twain and Elvis.

He is with his dog, Catfish, now—happy, and he finally knows just how the Bulldogs will do next year. I'm sure the good Lord, his momma, and his daddy met him at the gate with a big sign that says "Go Dawgs!"

I'll miss you, Bubba. The South will never be the same without you, but it is forever better because you were among us. You done good, Bubba! Goodbye.

Just thought you'd like to know...

Final Friends

Some may not think of Pensacola Beach in the heart of the Redneck Riviera as a typical small town, but it is. We have two gas stations, a general store for groceries, a hardware store that is opening soon, two churches (one Protestant and one Catholic), a T-shirt shop, six restaurants, and thirty-eight bars... and people don't come here to get gas and groceries!

We live on a mail route, have an unofficial mayor, and we fish a lot. If you take away the tourism, we would just be "South Pensacola!" Of course, the only tourists that go to Pensacola are lost and are looking for Pensacola Beach, anyway. I love this small town, but it is not the beauty of the area, the industry, or the location that keeps me here; it is the people. Home is where the heart is, and my heart will be buried here.

We make several sets of friends during our lifetime. When we graduated from high school, we had friends we swore we'd keep in touch with and be with forever, but as time passed, we have not heard from them in many years. Then we make friends at our work, our job, our chosen profession, but when we make our money and head in other directions, we leave them behind. The final set of friends we have are those that come into our lives about midlife. These are the friends that will come to our funeral, our final friends. There may be a few holdovers from our youth and middle age, but mostly we find our final friends when we slow down enough to learn what real friendships are.

Real friends come to your house when you are out of town and nail the vinyl siding that is flapping in the wind about to tear loose and never mention it. They come and feed your pets while you are gone, so they can stay in their environment and not have to be boarded. They know when you are gone and if anyone is around your house that should not be, stop them and inquire as to why they are there. They know your boat, and when it breaks its mooring, they will go out into the sound and bring it back and re-moor it for you, or pull you off a sandbar, just to laugh at you for being there in the first place. They know when your mother is not doing well and ask about your children, even the ones that have disappointed you or are troubled. When you are sick, they leave you alone, once they know you are okay. Final friends in life really don't care how much money you have; they care only that they enjoy your company and have grown enough to look past your failures and see the current person you have become. They are not afraid to introduce you to their other friends and laugh with you and not at you. I am not talking about "bar buddies" or acquaintances you see only when you are partying, but those that are there when you don't want to be with anyone. I have always accepted my friends "in spite of their faults" and our final friends return the favor.

My life, in many ways, is just beginning. This comedian thing came late for me. I am just beginning a new career when I should be looking at slowing down and spending some of my money. I can follow this dream because I find myself in a place that my friends support me totally, look out for "my place" when I am gone, and love me for who I am and not what I do. Time never seems to affect me, and when my final friends see me, it is just like yesterday we fished together and laughed.

I am thankful for my final home. A place where I can be with my final friends, surrounded by the beauty of God's beach and far enough away from the world to be in a small town worth living in.

Just thought you'd like to know...

CHAPTER 5

★ ★ ★

Big Ole Bubba

Just what is a "Bubba?" For one thing, Bubba has become the #1 nickname in the nation. It has also come to denote a particular stereotype of person. It's confusing for me. After all, my name is Bubba and I AM a Bubba. When someone calls me, I don't know if they want my attention or they are just describing me.

I have come to understand that "Bubba" is today an all-encompassing term of endearment for anything that is large, laid-back, and loveable! It comes from small children trying to say "Brother" when they are learning to speak. Bubba comes in all colors, shapes, genders, and sizes. Being a Bubba is a lifestyle, not a "look." Anyone can be a Bubba; it's just that most of them are big people. I have learned to explain it by telling others of the History of the John Bubbas—and there have been several. The first Bubba was John Wayne. Then came John Belushi, followed by John Candy, and today John Goodman is carrying the Bubba Banner high for all of us. See what I'm saying here? The loveable galoot, the big old teddy bear, the big man with a big heart, that everyone loves... just call me Bubba!

Being a Bubba

A lot of people like to think that us Bubbas talk funny. We don't talk funny; there are just a few things that we don't like to "finish" when we are talking. There are some things that we never say and a few things that we say every time we open our mouths! Bubba and Bubbette will affirm anything that they really believe in three times, as in, "Yep, I heard dat. Uh huh!" See what I'm talking about here? There are a few things that you will never hear Bubba or Bubbette say wherever you may encounter them.

For instance, you'll never hear Bubba say, "Hey, Bartender, give me a Zima!" I don't care if it is a southern beer, brewed in Memphis—Bubba

T. Bubba showing NASCAR Champion Jeff Gordon how to drive!

ain't gonna drink no beer the color of Vodka! You will never hear him say, "You can't feed that to the dog," or "Duct tape won't fix that," or "I need a hug!" If Bubba needs a hug, he'll do it himself! You won't hear him utter, "We're vegetarians," or "No kids in the back of the pickup; it ain't safe," or "I'll have the strawberries and granola, instead of the gravy and biscuits!" It just won't happen, like "I think too many deer heads spoil the décor," or "Trim the fat off my steak, please," or "I'll have the small bag of Jerky!" No way! You won't ever hear "Those tires are too big for that truck," or "Unsweetened tea tastes better," or "Cappuccino tastes better than Espresso!" If Bubba wants to pay $6 for a cup of coffee, it better have more than half the cup filled with Jack Daniels! You will never hear him yell out, "Checkmate," or "She's too young to be wearing that bikini," or "No more for me. Hell, I'm driving!" No way Jose! I don't think I have ever heard a Bubba say, "My feelings were hurt, you all," or "Hey, here's an episode of "The Man Show" that I ain't seen yet!"

But, while Bubba don't say or do certain things, he's still the glue that holds the entire country together, and one thing you'll always hear him say is, "God Bless America," "I love this country," and "Don't badmouth America, cause if you do you'll be walking on the fightin' side of me!" Yep, uh huh, I heard dat!

Just thought you'd like to know...

Why Men Are Proud to Be a Bubba

It ain't easy being a Bubba; it's like being Jewish. It's both a culture and a religion! Bubba is my name and I AM a Bubba, so now you clearly understand that statement! I am proud to be a Bubba, and if you wonder if you are eligible for membership, read on!

Why men are proud to be a Bubba:

- We can clean our fingernails with a pocket knife, a nail, or even a fork.

- We don't have to save ribbons of any kind.

- We can kill our own food.

- We get extra credit for the slightest act of kindness.

- If someone forgets to invite us to something, they can still be our friend.

- Car mechanics tell us the truth.

- We don't have to clean the house because the census taker is coming by!

- Grey hair and wrinkles, along with a little pot belly, only add character.

- We don't have to take a little gift every time we stop by to see someone; extra beer is enough.

- We don't have to shave anything below the neck!

- When our hair falls out, we can shave our heads and be "cool!"

- We don't need a hanky or napkin to blow our noses. We can do "snot rockets" and be cool!

- Phone conversations are over in twenty seconds flat.

- We laugh at anything we want, no matter who, where, or why!

- We don't have to be politically correct about anything.

- We can cuss, spit, or clear our throats without going outside.

- We are the masters of the remote control.

- We can refold road maps.

- We don't have to paint anything on our bodies ever!

- We can clip our toenails once a year and be groomed!

- We can make body sounds that will delight all within hearing range.

- We can run an outboard motor, a chain saw, and a meeting of any kind.

- We love old dogs and older whiskey, and understand politics.

- We don't have to go to church to talk to God; we can do it on the golf course, from a fishing boat, or the softball diamond. We go to church to make other people happy, like wives, children, and bosses.

- We never have to worry about the size of our butts being a factor on a first date.

- We drink beer and never have to worry about mixing drinks or what wine goes with what meat. Beer is like the color black—it goes with everything.

- And finally, being a Bubba is being a proud American. Bubbas don't think we need a "Missile Shield" around the USA. We could take Iran with the Mississippi National Guard, six flatbed wagons, and nine dozen ax handles in twenty minutes, if we had to. We don't need Star Wars; we need Star Bars. Everyone have a drink and be happy!

Just thought you'd like to know...

How to Weigh Yourself Properly

I have lost about 3,000 pounds since I was ten years old. I didn't ask for this weight and when I was a power lifter, I was even proud of it. I wasn't always built like a snowman; at one time I had somewhat of a manly shape, but when I was twenty-two years old, I wanted to lose some weight, so my doctor put me on a dehydrated-food diet. I ate nothing but

T. Bubba's famous belt buckle.

dehydrated food for six months, and then one day I got caught in the rain! I gained 143 pounds in ten minutes!

It was the ugliest thing you ever saw, laying on the side of the road with my clothes all ripped up and hanging off. I had to borrow a sheet from a nearby clothesline to get home!

However, I have learned how to "weigh" myself so that at least I feel better about it. Here are a few rules you might find helpful:

- Weigh yourself totally naked in the morning, even before you shower and get your hair wet. It is amazing how much weight you can lose just sleeping. Wet hair can add three pounds, so watch it!

- Take everything off before you weigh. Even your glasses. Poor eyesight can be a blessing here, trust me. Remove your wallet; some of those things can weigh up to four pounds. You ladies remove your panty hose; depending on your size, it could affect the weight. I think that Rosie O'Donnell's panty hose must weigh at least three pounds, so you can use her to gauge it.

- Go to the bathroom first. You don't want to weigh anything that you don't have to.

- Weigh with your arms spread open wide. It will divide the center of pressure on the scale and weigh less. And don't wave your arms around as that can add up to 20 pounds.

- Weigh yourself after haircut, and exhale all the air in your body. Air weighs a lot; that's why balloons fall to the floor when you blow them up.

- You must learn to mount the scales correctly. If you put a chair in front of the scales, place your weight on the chair back and let yourself down gently in the center of the scale. It will weigh a good two pounds less than it does when you just step on it.

- Don't use digital scales. They will scare the hell out of you as they go through their numbers. Use regular numbered scales and never use those that remember the weight the last time you weighed. Use your memory; the worse it is the better.

- Never use anyone else's scales. I have learned from experience they are all about fifteen pounds over in their weighing. I don't know why, but this is true.

I bought me a new blue suit last month. One day I yawned while standing at the bus stop and two people dropped letters into my mouth!

If you do all of the above, you will find that it makes you happier. You won't weigh less, but like those people that set their clocks and watches ten minutes earlier so they will be on time, it will give you false confidence; and after all, ain't we all after that one? Gotta go have a pizza now. I'm gonna weigh the pizza before I eat it and see if I gain the same amount after I am through eating it. I bet I weigh less, cause I know about this weighing thing.

Just thought you'd like to know...

Feelin' Heavy on Bubba's Beach

Well, it is summer again and this weight thing has given me the blues! Why can't I lose weight? I have tried all my life. Even as a kid I was huge; I tried to run away from home at seven years old and I had to take the truck route! I had a tricycle built for three. My first-grade school picture said, "continued on other side." When we played cowboys and Indians, I had to be the posse. I was too fat to play little league baseball, but the coach used me to draw the on-deck circle! I was standing in the middle of the street once at a junior high dance and a cop walked up to me and said, "Hey, break it up!" I was the original mold for the hula hoop! When we played hide and seek, I could only play seek! My graduation picture was taken by satellite! It was a hard childhood.

And it did not get any better when I went to college. I went to my first toga party and I had to use a belt to hold up the toga! I had more chins than a Chinese phonebook! I would go in the campus bakery and take all the numbers! My English teacher told me, "No man is an island, but you come pretty close." The only heavy reading I did was the bathroom scales. I went to a costume party once and just stuck a pinecone in my ear and went as the state of Georgia! I looked like a kangaroo with all the kids home! I was so lonely I got a dog, but I was so fat, one day I stepped on his tail and he died! I went out once to eat by myself and the waitress wanted to know if I wanted separate checks! I went to the beach once, but no one could swim while I was in the ocean; the beach disappeared and they all went home! Little children kept throwing water on me yelling, "Keep him wet or he will sunburn and it will kill him!" I graduated Suma Cuma Suppa Soona!!

Howdy from "Bubba's Beach" in the heart of the Redneck Riviera.

And it ain't getting any better as an adult. Last month I got a shoeshine and had to take the guy's word for it! I mean, "one size fits all" doesn't include me! I am the reason they went to the "one size fits most" tag. When I buy a car now, tilt steering wheels and six-way power seats are no longer an option! All the "all you can eat" restaurants have added "except Bubba" to the bottom of their signs. Last week it took me two trips to get through the revolving door at the Hilton. I just never met a meal that I didn't like! And my favorite food is seconds! I had to buy larger mirrors for my bedroom!

I bought me a new blue suit last month. One day I yawned while standing at the bus stop and two people dropped letters into my mouth! It is sad, folks. I took up horseback riding; the horse has lost twenty-five pounds so far. The first day the horse and I didn't go anywhere; his front feet couldn't touch the ground.

So, if you ever get on an elevator with me, you need to be going down. And if you ever see Old Bubba on the street, just throw me a sandwich. I am going out to Houston next week to teach George Foreman how to eat and I expect I will be gone for some time; so until then, always remember, "wet birds never fly at night."

Just thought you'd like to know...

What I Have Learned

There are lots of essays and e-mail these days by many people on the topics of "What I have learned." Some cute things from children. Some by "seasoned citizens" filled with wisdom. And some just too politically correct for me to read. So, I thought I'd write my own list of things I have learned as an older Bubba.

- I have learned that ice cream licked from my fist, the front of my shirt, or off the kitchen floor tastes just as good as from the cone or bowl.

- I have learned there is no way to make a woman permanently happy, but you can fool some of them most of the time.

- I know now that dogs are man's best friend and cats are God's way of telling us there is indeed a Satan.

- I have learned that all intelligent people sooner or later begin to listen to country music.

- I know your children never leave home; they just change addresses.

- I have learned that I can be angry without being cruel.

- I have learned that people who don't want to be my friend lose more than I do.

- I can't believe I'm still not the person I want to be... and though I may never become that person, I should not ever stop trying.

- I have learned God gave me the ability to make people laugh, and what a powerful gift that is.

- I have learned to say "I love you" to every man and woman I care for each time I leave them, for I may never see them again. Three times that has happened in my life and I cannot erase the memories.

- I have learned real love does not come in ages, kinds, or when expected!

- I have learned that just because some people don't love me all I want them to, it does not mean they don't love me all they are capable of.

- I have learned money does matter, even when it is not supposed to.

- I have learned I must live where I am happy and not where my work is.

- I have learned the older and uglier I get, the funnier I am; and that's good because God put me on planet Earth to make people laugh.

- I have learned most secrets were not worth learning about in the first place.

- I have learned "your son is your son until he takes a wife, and your daughter is your daughter for the rest of her life." I wish I had had a daughter; I think I would have been a kinder, gentler man today.

- And finally, I have learned time and distance cannot diminish true love. Only indifference can destroy it.

Just thought you'd like to know...

Diets

I went on a diet this month! So far I have lost twenty-two days! I lose weight, but it always comes back. My fat cells must have some kind of homing device. My doctor suggested I try running in place, and I said, "In place of what?" He slapped me and I paid him $75 and left! I exercise regularly, the same way February has twenty-nine days regularly. I went to the gym last week and the manager told me to get in shape. I told him, "Hey Bubba, round *is* a shape!" I slapped him and left! It is probably time to change my diet. I got a cholesterol test, and the results came back addressed to the family of the deceased. It said that they found "bacon!" I have eaten so many doughnuts; I now have honey-glazed arteries!

I really believe in exercise, but my body is more of an agnostic! I thought I was about the same weight I was in college, but the other day I pulled on an old pair of bell-bottom pants and they were real tight around the ankles! I know I should exercise, but my body has outlasted 22 cars and four boats! At least I don't have stress; some people get bent out of shape by life's little hassles. I let beer and chips get me out of shape. At least I can explain that at the Bubba meetings!

I am proud to be from the generation that smoked, ate anything we could fit into our mouth, drank

T. Bubba goofing with "Goober." Now that's country!

enough to float the *Queen Mary* on the Mississippi, and never exercised. People say we are a dying breed! I went to an equipment store the other day and told the clerk that I wanted to buy a machine to help my health; he told me to buy a respirator! I bought a fancy rowing machine and lost ten pounds dragging that thing up to my attic for storage.

I think God meant for me to be fat. Fat is good; it makes it nice to be close to another person without hurting yourself!

I give up. Love me the way I am, or just *like* me!

Just thought you'd like to know...

CHAPTER 6

★ ★ ★

Aging

I don't mind getting older when you consider the alternative! Birthdays bring age; I don't know why we celebrate them. Getting old is not for wussies; you gotta be strong and brave. I have pains in places I didn't know could hurt. And I don't get around as well as I used to, but then I don't have as much to do, either.

I think aging is a state of mind. I am enjoying it even if I don't want to! I can't wait to be that curmudgeon of a little old man that says what he wants to and farts in public just to see the reaction of people. I got an idea that I'm going to get to that point ahead of schedule, cause I am what I am. I can't wait. Bring it on; I'm ready!

Aging Ain't for Wussies

Life is always the way you see it. There is no other way to view it. You can say that you "look at life through other people's eyes," but we never can do that fully, as we are not them. We often fool ourselves into thinking that we do this, but if it were possible we would all be wondering who we really are after a while.

I see the world through Bubba's eyes. I am a Bubba and my name is Bubba, so it gets confusing to me at times. For instance, I never read the fine print on anything, as there just ain't no way you are ever going to like it. I never accept certified mail. When 'Lishous asked me why one day, I said, "Ain't never got no good news by certified mail," and it is the truth.

I never let my smile be my umbrella. The times I did, my butt got soaking wet. Besides, you can't hold a smile over your head; it just won't leave your face. The older I get, the less active I get. I think that is the way it is supposed to be; older people acting like young folks are stupid looking. The only three things I do more of with each passing year is urinate, attend funerals, and learn more about toe fungus than I ever wanted to know.

I hope we wake up in this country and begin to love our bodies again.

Senior life is not a sports car; it is a limo. Limos have wide seats and leg room. Sports cars have bucket seats, and the trouble with that is, not everyone has the same size bucket. When I get into my Corvette now, my butt pushes every button on the door and the console. It takes me ten minutes to realign the seats, the windows, the mirrors, and the convertible top just so I can leave the driveway! I have outgrown my car; now that is not something you hear every day!

I don't want to live forty more years. I can't imagine a society with sixty- to eighty-year-old women running around with all those sagging tattoos! I wonder what they are going to morph into? Why, a little lizard will become an alligator if placed on certain parts of the body! If I could just invent a tattoo eraser, I'd be rich in a few days, but I'd give free removals to all those women with tattoos on their buttocks and breasts, just to keep America beautiful.

I hope we wake up in this country and begin to love our bodies again. There is something sad about a person that feels that they have to inject ink in the shape of a dragon on their leg to be more attractive to someone or just drive a nail through their nose to stand out. What happened to just being funny or stronger or faster or smarter in order to "stand out?" Why do so many people feel that marking up their bodies is something that other people want to look at? I have had so many of them say, "Well, it's my body and my way of expressing myself!" Yeah, right, but I'm the one that has to look at it and wonder just what you were smoking when you painted the little hummingbird sucking the nectar out of a dagger dripping blood, and then make the decision as to whether to hire you or not. It is your body, it is your life, but don't ever make the mistake of thinking how you treat both of these things makes a difference only to you. Trust Ole Bubba on this one... How you lived your life, how you treated others, and how you made them feel about you WILL BE your life when you are gone from planet Earth, not how you felt about yourself.

Just thought you'd like to know...

What Is Wrong with the World?

I seem to have a lot of friends who are getting older. They don't look like they used to and I can't understand why. I look the same; why don't they? However, a few things are different. Have you noticed lately everything seems uphill from wherever you start? Even if I start at the top, it just seems uphill. I can't figure this out. Stairs are steeper, groceries are heavier even though I'm not eating any more, and everything is farther away. My remote went out last night and the TV was at least a block away from my sofa.

I went out for a walk down the street where I live yesterday and was dumbfounded to discover how much longer it had become! I think they

The great George Jones and T. Bubba hamming it up at the Grand Ole Opry.

made the lots larger somehow and the houses further apart. It seems to me people are more edgy these days, and the young people just make you want to slap them; everyone seems to bother me more. It used to be that people would say something to me and talk so as I could understand them the first time. Why are people just mumbling everything today? I think they are much less mature than I was at their age, and people my age seem to be so much older than I am. When I got married last month, I had friends I had not seen in twenty years and most of them didn't recognize me. It was sad to see that their eyesight had gotten so bad! They were all bald, bent over, and walked so slow, and some of them were years younger than me! I guess their memories are going too! I looked in the mirror today and even the mirrors are warping things out of shape. I can't even buy a good mirror these days!

The quality is gone out of everything. Even my pants don't hold up like they used to. I got a run in my blue jeans today and that was just too much for me. I guess I'll have to go to stretch pants for a good fit. The jeans manufacturers have just lost touch with sizes. Have we gone to metric in jeans? Why, I can't even get a size 48 around me anymore, and a 32 length is now a 30!! I think that they are trying to save material and quality!

The people that make scales are the same way! My scale won't even register my weight; it just keeps coming up "Error." What the hell does "error" mean? How can my weight be an error? I guess I'll have to get me an old scale that isn't digital and can give me the correct weight. The telephone book has gone to pot as well. The print is so small that I have to put the page on my copy machine and enlarge it to read it nowadays. Why are they doing this? Even my shoes are such poor quality they busted out on both sides yesterday, I'm going to have to live in thongs for the rest of my life, and they look so funny in the winter with socks!

I don't know what has gone wrong with the world, but I think that us more mature folks had better sound the alarm soon or soon the entire world will be falling apart. There is just no quality left in the country! I would call my congressman, if I could read the dial on the phone!

Just thought you'd like to know...

The Over-Fifty Advantage

There are several advantages of being over fifty. I hurt in places I didn't know existed, and my skin is all trying to reach my knees as fast as it can, but there are a few real perks! In this time of war and terrorism, kidnappers are not very interested in me; and if they ever did catch me and hold me for ransom, they would release me when they had to feed me. In a fire no one expects me to run into a burning building. The last time I ran I had hair on my head. I don't run anywhere anymore. People call me at 11 a.m. and ask, "Did I wake you up?" It is a lot more respectful to take naps. No one views me as a hypochondriac any longer; they know I must be sick with something! I have learned everything I can the "hard way," and I now know how to do it the best way first. Most of the things I buy now I will have the rest of my life. That's cool. I can live with less sex, but I need more love. When people talk to me about their operations, I now know what they are talking about.

Pension plans are making more sense to me, and when I have a wild party my neighbors don't even know about it! Speed limits are no longer a challenge, and I know that I can get there in traffic within two to three minutes of ETA by doing under the speed limit. I still have a Corvette, but I use it now to attract looks only! I no longer have to hold my stomach in, because I'm over fifty and I'm supposed to have a little pouch! I know all the music in the elevator and can even sing along; that bothers the under-twenties and surprises the over-thirties! I'm beginning to collect from my health plan and I don't feel like I'm paying all that money out for nothing! I can tell all my secrets to my buddies because they won't remember them anyway!

I no longer have to hold my stomach in, because I'm over fifty and I'm supposed to have a little pouch!

And finally, I don't care what people think of how I dress, how I talk, how I drive, or how I smell. I'm over fifty, so get used to it! I'm having a ball and I can't wait for seventy! I'm going to be a lot more ornery, and when I hit eighty, totally unbearable!

Just thought you'd like to know...

Bubba's Changing World

I never thought I'd live this long. I used to think that the brave and beautiful died young, and I just knew I'd die by age thirty, cause there was not a man any more brave and beautiful than I. Instead I just got old, fat, and ugly, and now I may live forever! I find constant change in my life. A new language erupts every three years and words I never thought would affect my life, have. I'm doing the best I can, but I fear I'm lagging and I hate to lag. I have to sag, but I don't have to lag. I never thought I'd ever stay in touch with my family by e-mail, and if someone doesn't have a computer, they don't even get a Christmas card from me anymore! I have a list of thirty-five phone numbers to reach a family of five people. I pull in my own driveway and phone 'Lishous to see if she is in the house to come and help me with the groceries. I wonder just when we will run out of numbers for all these phones, faxes, pagers, and such. The universe just doesn't have that many numbers, does it? I know a grandmother that asked her son to send her a JPEG file of her new grandson, so she could make a screen saver! Whatever happened to snapshots? I learned ten years ago that a nanosecond is the time between the time I buy my computer and it becomes obsolete!

When I was a boy, and anyone called after 6 p.m., my grandparents didn't even answer the phone. Why, who would be calling at that late hour, indeed? If it was important, they'd call back the next day! The telephone was an interruption to our lives. Today we have them surgically installed on our hips—why, to miss a call would be disaster.

Yesterday I tried to enter my password into my microwave! Fed-Ex is already too slow, and the post office is a total joke. Why, three days to deliver a letter is two and a half days too slow. I think in my lifetime I will see the post office cease to exist. No one ever tells me a joke anymore that I have not already gotten from e-mail. I want a microwave fireplace, so I can enjoy an entire evening before the fire in about six minutes, but I can't find one on the Internet. Today I went online before I had coffee, and my wife had already been online for an hour. I checked my e-mail on the way back from the bathroom this morning at 3:30 a.m., and have considered having a screen installed on the front of my sink, so while I sit on the throne, I can talk to my manager in Nashville! Last week I tried to forward the doorbell when it rang, and I won't even get into using real money anymore—that's another article. Lord, slow me down. Unless I can get to heaven on the world wide web, and the angels have a Web site, then I'd rather just as soon get into that chat room and I won't have to ever go!

Just thought you'd like to know...

CHAPTER 7

★ ★ ★

Animals

I have had animals as a part of my life as long as I can remember. I have had every pet you can imagine, except snakes. There are only two things in the world I am "crap-in-my-pants" afraid of, and both of them are snakes. My wife, Lishous, and I feel differently about pets. She lives with them; I like them outside. Houses are for people; yards are for pets. When we married a few years ago, she had two cats, Beezlebub and Satan. I have a great dog, Rolex (I named him that because he is a "watch" dog), and two parrots—Abbub (Bubba backwards), an African grey, and Amigo, a double yellowhead. After living together for a year, we made a vow. When they all die, that is it! No more pets! I think we both mean it. Maybe it's time for a goldfish—one that runs on batteries. I love animals, but enough is enough!!

Bubba and the Bear

I have lived an exciting life. Things just seem to happen to me. I have seen the world twice, saw Elvis three times, met five presidents—and once

I played pool with a king. But last night was one event I want to forget. I am prone to embellishment at times. It's what I do... how I make people laugh. But this is a true story... totally.

I came home after several adult beverages at one of my favorite island oasis watering holes, pulled my motorcycle up into the driveway, and heard my dog Rolex barking very loud, growling and howling like I had never heard him before. I went around the side of the house to see what the commotion was. In the dark I passed a bush that all of a sudden... moved! I know I had not been "over-served," as I was on my Gold Wing motorcycle and I never ride intoxicated. I AM crazy... but I ain't stupid. I knew I was not "seeing things" as I bent over and walked toward the "bush" to further investigate this phenomenon. I got about three feet from it and it moved again, this time very fast. I thought it was another dog, so I "stomped" at it and hollered to scare it away. Just as I got close enough to hit it with the palm frond I had picked up in the yard, he shook his fur. Saltwater went all over me—and that made me mad, so I yelled at it again.

This time the "thing" turned and let out a very loud growl. All I could see was teeth and a tongue big and close! In fact, the thing was so close to me that I felt its breath. It must have eaten a skunk that day for lunch, because his breath would have knocked a buzzard off a dookie wagon!

Something told me this was not a "big dog," but something from Dante's Inferno sent to eat me! I jumped at least four feet straight up into the air and then it ran into the street right under a street lamp next to my house!

I was still up in the air, when I saw a BEAR! A large bear and it was not happy with me. A big bear, on an island in the Gulf of Mexico, and I was sober! The bear began to lumber down the street. When I hit the ground, I began to run after it. Now folks, I was about twenty yards down the street when the voice of the "God of all Bubbas" came into my head and said to me, "Bubba, you are chasing a bear with a rotten palm frond in your hand." The thought had not occurred to me as to what I would do with it if I caught up with it. I stopped, realized I was the dumbest person on the planet at that moment, and ran into my house—which was not easy in itself; my legs were not working too well and I had this large lump in the rear of my pants that prohibited my regular stride! I did not open the door first; I just went in. The carpenters are coming next Monday to re-place the door.

I grabbed the phone and called the Ranger Station. Yes, a Ranger Sta-tion. Bubba's Beach is located between a national park and a state park. I knew everyone at the Sheriff's Department and thought maybe the rang-ers would think I was not just a drunk and seeing "pink elephants." When the ranger answered at 1:33 a.m., I yelled, "This is Bubba, and I just saw a bear in my yard!" There was a long period of total silence. Then the ranger said, "You are who, and you saw a what?" I said, "Bubba, and I saw a wet bear with bad breath in my yard. I ran him down the street and he ain't happy." The ranger said, "Okay, thanks for the call."

"Thanks for the call." That was it! I knew I had not connected and they thought it was a crank call so I called the Sheriff's Department. How-ever, as I went back in the yard with my 12-guage shotgun, loaded with Skeet loads that would only have made the bear mad if I shot him with it, a sheriff's car was in front of my house, lights flashing, deputy with a big gun, the whole nine yards. Yes, someone had taken me seriously... finally. Lights were beginning to come on at my neighbors' and the deputy pulled up, let the passenger window down, and asked "Bubba, did you call in a bear sighting?" He was smiling like he knew I was up to one of my pranks and looking me over for empty beer bottles and dirt on my knees from possibly crawling home. He said, with a large sly smile, "Now Bubba, was it a little bear, or a big bear?" Was it like a Yogi Bear or a Care Bear? At that moment, I knew he did not believe me either and I wished I had lived my life totally different, maybe been a minister or little league coach so he would have a better attitude toward me!

To make matters worse, at this very moment my wife drives up. Now the lady of my life is here, I am no longer alone, and I have an ally that will believe me for sure. She walked up, looked the situation over, blue and red lights bouncing off her face, looked at the deputy, and asked, "What has he done now?" I was all alone, not a friend in sight, just another Bubba that everyone thought had at last totally left his mind. Just then, the radio cracked in the deputy's car and dispatch yelled, "Hey, Bubba's not making it up; we just got two other calls. There IS a large bear running down Panferio Drive, headed for Via de Luna!" HA! I was vindicated! I was a hero! I looked them both in the face and said, "See, now you can both kiss my wide white butt!" The deputy shot off and Tarsha had that look on her face she has when she can't figure out where she lost her sunglasses and they are on her forehead!

The bear then went into the lobby of the Clarion Hotel, scared the hell out of a few "tourons" from Ohio, tried to climb a piling on the new Gulf pier, and finally sought refuge in the Cross Dune, where the rangers shot him with a tranquilizer dart and took him off to bear heaven.

Just then, the radio cracked in the deputy's car and dispatch yelled, "Hey, Bubba's not making it up! There IS a large bear running down Panferio Drive!"

To say the least, it took me days to get my heart back into my chest and to realize how close I had come to being bear dessert. The next morning I found the tracks in my backyard coming out of the bay and toward my house. Senior Deputy Gunn at the substation told me it was a male black bear, about 250 pounds, and was looking for a female to mate with. If the bear had asked me, I would have told him there was not a female on the entire island that was available for mating! While I have been out of circulation since Lishous applied the tourniquet, some things never change!!

I also know now why he ran from me as well. He had never seen anything as big as me. I outweigh him seventy pounds and got three inches on him. I am probably bigger than his momma and his daddy. He also could have caught a smell of me as well, and that would have made anyone run! So, the next time I tell you I saw anything, a UFO, a conservative democrat or a white alligator, believe me. Okay?

Just thought you'd like to know...

Dog Notice for Front Door

I have a dog; his name is Rolex. I named him that because he's a "watch" dog! He is a Golden "Reliever" and part human. I have this notice on my front door! I love this dog; he is my pal and the only thing I know on planet Earth that loves me "unconditionally." The following sign has been on my front door for years:

- The dog lives here; you don't!

- If you don't want dog hair on your clothes, stay off the furniture!

- Yes, he has some disgusting habits. So do I and so do you. What's your point?

- If he sniffs your crotch, please feel free to sniff his.

- If he licks you, don't scold him; it's his way of saying "welcome."

- Don't expect him to do any tricks; putting up with humans is a full-time job for him.

- If he looks at you funny, understand that I may do the same thing!

- I like him a lot better than most people. To you he's a dog. To me he's an adopted boy, who is short, hairy, walks on all fours, and doesn't speak clearly. I have no problem with any of these things! If you do, go away!

Dogs are better than children: they eat less, don't ask for money all the time, are easier to train, usually come when called, never drive your car, don't hang out with drug-using friends, don't smoke or drink, don't worry about whether they have the latest fashions, don't wear your clothes, don't need a gazillion dollars for college, and if they get pregnant you can sell the puppies! The same applies for my wife's cat, except she will ignore you... until you're asleep!!

I just thought you would like to know...

Dog Dreams

My dog Rolex was dreaming the other day. I was sitting next to the microwave oven when lightning hit our house, and for the next six minutes I could see what Rolex was dreaming about. It could happen, you know. Anyway, I was sitting there listening to his dreams and I thought I'd share them with you. Your dog may just be having the same dreams.

He dreamed, "I wonder if there are any fireplugs in heaven?" Then he thought of me and said, "Bubba, how come you always tell me I smell like a wet dog, and when I go to smell you, you hit me with the newspaper? 'Why do you always use the bathroom in my big blue water bowl; can't

you get your own bowl? How come there are no cars named after dogs? We got cars named after every other animal in the world, but only one after a dog. That Porsche Boxer thing is just too weak. I'm talking about an SUV Bulldog, or a Jeep Mastiff, something that would make a statement."

"If I come back to earth as a human, is that a good or bad thing? Seems to me, dogs have it a lot better. We dogs under-stand human verbal instruc-

Country music superstar Toby Keith shows T. Bubba "Who's ya Daddy?"

tions, hand signals, whistles, horns, clickers, beepers, invisible fences, and Frisbee flight paths. Just what the hell does Bubba understand? So far, all I have figured out is that he knows the stove works and how to get stains out of his underwear."

"I wonder if there are dogs on other planets and why no dog ever howls back when I howl. Am I the only howler on earth? Why does Bubba get the newspaper every morning when I could do that and save him that long trip to the end of the driveway? I wonder if it is because I tried to read the thing last time and it made him mad. What real purpose do cats serve on earth? I have lived with two for several years now and I have never seen anything more useless than a cat. Not one time have either of them ever done anything for anyone other than themselves. They eat their fur and puke it up. How stupid is that? They meow at nothing and wonder why we don't understand. They sit and stare at the sun and feel like everyone should join them. Cats leave fur everywhere. It's hard to breathe in here sometimes. Why don't they lick the floor? There is more fur there than on their bodies. Then they could puke up larger fur balls and enjoy the possibility of death. Cats suck! I wonder if, when I get to heaven, I might could get my testicles back. I don't know why 'Lishous had them cut off. They were not bothering anyone and I enjoyed them. I hope God understands and gives them back to me."

"I wonder why everyone in this house loves to put their hands on my head and pat me. Don't they know that is a stupid thing to do? How about if they did that to themselves? I bet they would reconsider doing it to us. My head hurts from all the pats when company comes; try the back end sometimes."

"I don't know why humans don't lick themselves. Licking is fun and relieves stress. If they could lick themselves, they would have no need for shrinks and doctors, and they'd be a lot cleaner." And finally. "I'm going to be more patient with Bubba and do better with him in the future. He's a slow learner, but he has a good heart, and I could do worse."

Just thought you'd like know...

Pig Farts Can Be Lethal

Recently an airliner heading to South Africa had to make an emergency landing in England. It seems that seventy-two pigs being transported in the luggage compartment had set off the fire alarm. I'm not making this up! It is an AP and UPI story! I couldn't write anything this funny! I ain't that good!

I began to wonder several things when I read this. I wondered what a flatulent pig sells for in South Africa. I wondered if a white person from South Africa moves to America, will he be called an African American? How did the "pig gas" set off a fire alarm? And what do you call "pig gas" anyway? Pig-ulence? I wondered if pigs ever say to one another, "Pull my hoof." What is going on here? You know the pigs are laughing their flatulent little hammies off,... "Hey Bubba, we landed a 747 with farts, how cool is that?"

It seems, upon further investigation (someone has to do these things), the pigs were all stud pigs headed to South Africa for breeding. Not a bad life, if you can stand the flatulence! Stud pigs drink a lot of beer and punch each other in the arms and stud for a living! This has led directly to Gloria Steinem saying that "all men are pigs!"

And what do you call "pig gas" anyway? Pig-ulence?

It seems that the combination of pig gas, pig urine, and pig body heat created some sort of biological chain reaction that set off the alarm. My god, it is a wonder that any of the pigs lived, but then, stud pigs are tough! I would like to have seen the look on the face of the man that opened the door first! He must still be home scrubbing his skin and wondering if he will ever smell the same again! He never knew what hit him!

So, what have we learned from this? First, this airline does not ever want to transport cows! When the airline asks you if you packed your own bags, you have the right to ask if there are any flatulent pigs onboard! A pig gets gas when it is confined in an airplane and gives us gas when it is put into country sausage! Now we know why we "pickle" pig's feet before we eat them! And finally, stud pigs produce more flatulence than female pigs, because that's the way males are; it is a law of nature.

I love my job!

Just thought you'd like to know...

Reincarnation

I've been pondering on this reincarnation thing. If there is anything to it, I want to come back as a bear. I used to want to be an eagle, but I just can't eat rats and feel good about it.

Yep, I want to come back as a bear. A bear sleeps for six months at a time. I can deal with that. I like to sleep. It's the best of both worlds; you can be unconscious and alive at the same time, and nobody dares wake you up—not unless they are crazy.

If I came back as Mama Bear, that would be cool; I ain't never been a woman. Bears get pregnant, sleep for six months, and then give birth to a baby the size of a walnut. That completely saves that six- to ten-pound baby thing that would scare most men to death. The baby bear sleeps with you and when you wake up, it's nearly half grown... Now, that's the way to have a baby! If you are a bear, your wife expects you to wake up growling and have a huge beer belly, hairy legs, and hairy back. She expects you to fish all day and if anything makes you mad, you just beat the hell out of it! Yes, I think that the bears are the Bubbas of the animal world.

If I come back as a bear, I want to be a Kodiak bear, not a Polar bear. All Polar bears are left handed (that's the truth), and I can't do anything with my left hand but eat. A big old Kodiak bear, about twelve feet tall, 2,007 pounds, and teeth the size and shape of icicles; then let's see "WHO'S YER BUBBA!!"

Yep, gonna come back as a bear...

Just thought you'd like to know...

Rolex's Resolutions

My dog Rolex is part human. He was dreaming last night and his dreams spilled out onto the tile floor and I was able to read them. He is trying to be better with these resolutions. I just thought I would share them with you.

- I will not play tug-of-war with Bubba's underwear when he's on the toilet.

- I will not chase the garbage collector as he is NOT stealing our stuff.

- I will not need to suddenly stand straight up when I'm lying under the coffee table.

- I will not roll my toys behind the fridge.

- I must shake the saltwater out of my fur BEFORE entering the house.

Country music star and actor Tim McGraw with T. Bubba "early on."

- I will not eat the cats' food, before or after they eat it.

- I will stop trying to find the few remaining pieces of clean carpet in the house when I am about to throw up.

- I will not roll on dead seagulls, fish, crabs, or jellyfish and then go rub on Bubba.

- I will not lick Bubba's face after eating cat poop again. It was fun, but it was wrong, just wrong!!

- "Kitty box crunchies" are not food.

- I will not eat any more socks and then redeposit them in the backyard after processing.

- I will not drink the blue water from the big bowl in the bathroom ever again.

- I will not chew Bubba's toothbrush and not tell him!

- I will not chew crayons or pens, especially not the red ones, or Tarsha will think I am hemorrhaging again.

- When in the car, I will not insist on having the window rolled down when it's raining outside.

- We do not have a doorbell. I will not bark each time I hear one on TV.

- The sofa is not a face towel. Neither are Bubba's bare feet.

- My head does not belong in the refrigerator.

- I will try to go and get everything Bubba throws. It is my job, why I am here, and he needs the company; he has so few friends!

- I will not hold the cat down and lick its belly anymore. It took me a week to get the fur out of my teeth, and the cat did not like it much either!

- I will try never again to poop in the cat's box and watch Bubba look for a tiger in the house!

Just thought you'd like to know...

Inside Pets

My wife Bubba-Lishous has taken my dog Rolex (I named him that because he's a "watch" dog) and turned him into a house dog. The only reason my former, he-man, outside, retrieving champion dog is not a lap dog is because he weighs nearly 100 pounds. If she could get him on her lap, I'm sure he'd pretty much be a lap dog. When she moved in and began to "redo" my house into a zoo, I looked the other way. I just figured, two cats, two parrots, a big dog, and a little woman—all came with the package, and I took it all in stride. But the process nearly killed me. When Rolex and the cats came inside, the dialog went something like this:

- Dogs are <u>never</u> permitted in the house! The dog stays outside, under the shed, in a self-made hole that is cool, out of the sun, and of his own making. He is quite happy there! He loves it and won't go into a doghouse of any kind.

- Okay, the dog can enter the house, but <u>only</u> for short visits or if he is ill.

- Inside the house, the dog is <u>not allowed</u> to run free and is confined to a comfortable, very large room that I paid $20,000 for. His food is there, it is a tile floor, and he is happy there with the cats and the parrot!

- Okay, the dog can come inside for short visits on the carpet, but the dog is <u>never</u> allowed on the furniture.

- Okay, the dog can get on the old furniture, but not the <u>new</u> furniture.

- Okay, the dog can get up on the new furniture because now it looks like the old furniture, because the cat has scratched it, dookied on it, and drooled on it to the point that we'll sell the whole damn works and buy new furniture... upon which the dog will most definitely <u>not</u> be allowed.

- No, I'm not cleaning up the dog poop. You wanted him in the house, you go get the shovel and bury it, then mop the floor, and fumigate the entire house.

- The dog or the cat <u>never</u> sleeps in the bedroom. Period!

- Okay, the dog and cat can sleep at the foot of the bed, on your side, <u>not</u> mine!

- Okay, the cat can sleep alongside you, but she's <u>not</u> allowed under the covers.

- No, I will not check out the dog's snoring with the vet. You wanted him in here, you put up with the snoring. I don't care if he shakes the windows. It doesn't seem to bother the cat. Get used to it; she did.

- Okay, the dog can sleep and snore and have nightmares in the bedroom, but he's <u>not</u> to come in and sleep on the couch in the living room, where I'm now sleeping. That's just not fair.

- No, I won't sleep with you, or your cat fur pillows and red dog hair rugs in the bedroom. If you want to see me, I'll be in the guest bedroom with the towels stuffed under the door.

- And finally, yes, I love you, even if I can't find you in the house any longer! Let's get a room at a hotel on the beach and make love... one that doesn't allow animals would be nice!

Just thought you'd like to know...

CHAPTER 8

Sports

Bubba and Bubbette love sports. It's the competition. We like to compete in everything we do. We want to be first. We want to lead the pack, to never lag behind; and sports is a way to keep score. Bubba knows that sports of all types are the best way for children to build character and learn lessons that will serve them the rest of their lives. I am the envy of all my friends: I married a "jock!" 'Lishous was a soccer goalie, played second base in softball, was forward on the basketball team, and is in every sports fantasy team on the Internet. She received a soccer scholarship out of high school, and her two brothers, Jeff and Joel, her sister Heidi, and even her mother were all athletes in a variety of sports. So, when the game is coming on, I have to fight for the best seat in front of the TV, and we bleed Garnett and Gold as serious Florida State football fans. I have always said, "I grabbed a football and ran out of poverty with it." Football gave me a college education and made me popular. I had to learn how to be a gentleman. I got to run with the "other half" and learned how to be a team player, all because of football, track and field, baseball, and being blessed, at Long Beach, Mississippi High School, with a 275-pound body that could move like a gazelle. Sports can be a way out for a lot of kids that don't have any other way. Just remember this: A million-dollar body won't take you far in life with a twenty-dollar mind!

Football North and South

Football is the true religion of the Southland!

It is different here than in the North. New Englanders hardly have a Division One football team in the entire rock pile up there. They don't play the same game we do. Just ask heavily favored Ohio State who fully expected to beat the Florida Gators in a national championship—only they got their butts kicked up and down the field. We play differently in the south. That is why Northern teams hardly ever beat Southern teams. I understand that it did happen once, but I wasn't born yet, so it don't count.

Here are a few subtle differences in the game here and up there, according to my friends at the University of Alabama:

Up North, fathers expect their daughters to understand Sylvia Plath

T. Bubba the linebacker. It was 1965 at Perkinston Jr. College and T. Bubba was 6'1" and 285 lbs.

and Maya Angelou. In the South, fathers expect their daughters to understand the "nickel defense" and what a "squib kick" is.

Dressing to attend a game is different as well for women. Northern women have a Chapstick in their back pocket along with a $20 bill. Here, women have a leather backpack with three lipsticks, waterproof mascara, hairbrush, breath mints, and a fifth of Southern Comfort. They don't carry money; that is what dates are for!

Alumni functions are different as well. Northern fans take their prospects on sailing trips and play golf with members of the firm; in the South we take our future college players on hunting trips with alumni that played in the NFL and make sure their mommas get a better house to live in.

Cheerleaders are different as well. Up North they look like Russian gymnasts and PETA activists. Down South cheerleaders look like Miss America in a bikini. The male cheerleaders up North look like Pee Wee Herman in drag; here they look like Jose Canseco and Michael Jordan.

The Homecoming queens are far different as well, notwithstanding the obvious difference in size. The Northern queen is a Diversity Studies major; the Southern queen is Miss USA looking for a degree in MRS.

The campus decor is very different. In the North the campus will be laden with busts of alumni politicians, poets, and university presidents. In the South you will find statues of Heisman Trophy winners, Congressional Medal of Honor recipients, and national championship banners. Down here you will find heroes like Paul "Bear"Bryant, Bobby Bowden, Hershal Walker, Bobby Bowden, Bo Jackson, and did I mention Bobby Bowden!!

Buying tickets for the games is easy in the North; you just walk up to the gate on game day, get a ticket, and go in. In the South, you write a check for a $10,000 donation just to get on the waiting list for an end zone seat, fifteen years in advance. Season tickets here are handed down in wills to heirs that would sue to get them!

Parking is a hoot as well. In the North you park your car next to the stadium on game day and go in. In the South the real faithful arrive on Wednesday, in a motor home with fifty-five people in it, begin drinking, and fire up the grill they towed behind the motor home. By game time on Saturday, they are ready to invade Iraq if they have to. They haven't showered in three days; they are drunk and could eat the bark off a pine tree. After the game Saturday, we then drive to the closest professional team and do it all over again.

When the National Anthem is played, half of the people in the half-filled stadium up North stand up and only about 40 percent even sing. In the South, 100 percent of the fans stand up, with the other 22,000 outside the stadium listening on the radio just to be a part of the atmosphere, and all sing in perfect three-part harmony! The one exception I have seen recently is Rutgers, but it took a coach from Miami to get them to understand the game and how to sing and win!

After the first score in the North they clap, mostly with mittens on. In the South, cannons are fired; fireworks go off, there is hugging and kissing, horses run around the field, and babies are thrown in the air, finished off with a swig of homemade whiskey!

Up North, the stadium is empty way before the game ends. Alumni leave early to be on time for their dinner reservations at the club, and students leave to make it back to Starbucks for discussions on global warming. In the South, kegs are repacked in ice at the fraternity houses. In parking lots, racks of ribs and whole pigs go on the smoker while somebody goes to the nearest package store for more bourbon. Planning begins for next week's tailgating party and game as people listen to the postgame show from the locker room and relive every great moment of the game like it never happened. They get ready for the next three-day workweek, or five if it is an "away game."

Bowl games are different as well in the North. If your school happens to make one, you watch part of it on TV. In the South, it's an eight-day drinking holiday; attendance required even if you don't have tickets, and 90 percent of every household is gathered around the TV with food, banners, signs, and lots of love. It's the South against all the rest of the country, and by God, we better win!

I played the game, in high school and at a small college. I played it until I couldn't walk anymore. My sons both played it; I missed four games in twelve years with them. It teaches more lessons on "how to live life" than anything else. I love the game. It is part of my culture, and I apologize to no one for it. So, kick it off and let's get on with it. Go 'Noles and God bless Bobby Bowden!

Just thought you'd like to know...

Bubba and the Old Golfer

I was waiting for my buddy Buster to show up to complete our foursome at Tiger Point Country Club recently. Buster took up golf recently and he is trying to shoot his weight!

He didn't show, and this old man who looked like he might need help to walk back to the clubhouse asked if he could join us. He said, "Sure, I play a little. You don't mind if I walk, do you? It helps my rheumatism." I told him that we played a fast game, and he said he'd try to keep up! I told him that we played for money, and he said that would be fine, that he may have to give us a check, but he was good for it!!

Not being able to discourage him, we began the first nine! He beat us all like a drum! Right down the middle, short, but letting the irons work for him! On the back nine, he took all our money and just embarrassed us. We wanted to play another nine, but he said he wanted to go do some drinking in the club. He did buy the first round and then he drank us under the table! He drank two to my one and wondered if something was wrong with me! He ate two Bar-B-Q sandwiches and four beers to wash it all

T. Bubba and pal Vince Gill at the "Vinny Golf Event."

down and said that he felt sluggish today because he had missed his work-out yesterday! I wanted to slap him!

Instead, I asked, "You old codger, you took all our money, you beat us 10 strokes per nine, and you drank us under the table. Doesn't old age have any disadvantage at all?"

He thought for a minute and said, "Yeah, I can think of one. This morning when I woke up, I asked my wife to make love and she said, "What, after six times last night?' You see... When you get old, your memory begins to slip a bit!!"

I hate old people!

Just thought you'd like to know...

Fishing

I love to fish. I fish sometimes just to get away from people. I like to fish alone; I can fish and ponder. Today I pondered about why fishing could be better than sex. I am not saying that it IS better than sex, but it could be in certain cases. I met a man on the pier today and he told me that fishing was better than sex because no matter how much whiskey you drink, you could still fish! That got me to pondering even more. After I caught my limit, I stopped by the Sand Shaker bar to discuss this fully with the collective wisdom of people like me. We came up with the following list:

- You don't have to hide your fishing magazines.

- Your fishing partner doesn't mind if you fish with others once in a while.

- A limp rod is still useful while fishing.

- It is perfectly acceptable to pay a professional to fish with you.

- You can take videos of fishing and show them to your neighbors.

- It is respectable to fish with a total stranger and you don't have to worry about what you catch.

- It is okay to have a favorite fishing hole and share it with your friend.

- You won't go blind if you fish by yourself.

- There are no fishing-transmitted diseases.

- If you want to watch fishing on television, you don't have to use pay-per-view!

- Nobody expects you to fish with the same partner for the rest of your life.

- You can sleep and fish at the same time!

- And finally, never take just one baptist fishing with you... he'll drink all your beer. Take two and neither one of them will drink one single beer.

Just thought you'd like to know...

CHAPTER 9

Bubba on the Sexes

I love women, and for some strange unexplainable reason, women have always loved me. I think it is because I make them laugh. When you make anyone laugh, you are "one" with them, if even for a moment. Laughter is needed to understand the difference between the sexes. Here are a few laughs for you!!

Things Women Need to Know

I love women, but sometimes I don't understand them. Women confuse me. Here are a few things that any woman that knows me or a fellow Bubba should know! These hints will help you bond with us and we will be happy; then you will get everything you want in life. Simple, right?

Read and learn...

- Never buy a new brand of beer because "it was on sale." You know what I drink; I don't bring you cheap Kool-Aid.

- Beer has an expiration date just like milk; learn to read it.

- If we're in the backyard and the TV in the den is on, that doesn't mean we're not watching it. We can watch TV and do at least five other things. It's the only multi-tasking we know how to do.

- Don't tell anyone we can't afford a new car. Tell them we don't want one, and never tell them you want one.

- Whenever possible, when I'm watching "the game," please try to say whatever you have to say during commercials. This will help in communications a lot better.

- Only wearing your new lingerie once does not send the message that you need more. It tells us lingerie is a bad investment. If you don't wear it now, you may not be able to later on. Wear it out, and we'll buy you more. If it don't cling, pitch it with the old underwear.

- Don't feel compelled to tell us how all the people in your stories are related to one another: We don't care. We're just nodding,

"Bubba-Lishous"—Bubba's wife and a very patient woman.

waiting for the punch line. Make sure each story has an ending and tell us when you are through talking; it is the only way we can tell! Then we know it is our time to talk.

- When the waiter asks if everything's okay, a simple "Yes" is fine. I don't want to know him and I don't care if he is going to college or has sick kids. He is just trying to enlarge his tip; get a clue. And oh yeah, 18 percent is more than enough. If the owner wants me to pay his employees, instead of him doing it himself, I can find another place to eat. Tipping is an ego trip for the tipper.

- What do you mean, "leering?" I am just looking at a beautiful thing. Don't you look at beautiful things? Just because I'm on a diet don't mean that I can't look at the menu! A really secure wife would actually point out things to leer at that we might miss otherwise.

- When I'm turning the wheel and the car is nosing onto the off ramp, saying "Oh, this is our exit, Honey" is not really necessary.

- Stop pointing out landmarks after I have passed them. Some men have developed whiplash traveling with women.

- When you're not around, I belch so loudly I even appall myself. I also pass gas and laugh at it, when it is especially odd sounding, so be grateful I have learned to enjoy myself without you. This way I'm not out leering at beautiful things.

- The temperature in the cave will be my responsibility. It will be slightly to moderately cooler than you want it. Learn to wear sweaters and sweatshirts. The air conditioner unit is there to use, not for display. No, I will not remove the iron box the thermostat is located in nor will I give you a key.

- ESPN Sports starts at 10:00 p.m. and runs one hour. This is an excellent time for you to pay bills, put laundry in the dryer, or talk to your sister. Just don't plan anything and you won't be upset when I watch it.

- Is it too much to ask to have the bra match the underwear? And that old hockey jersey is very sexy, let me tell you.

- I don't care, but friends are asking if we see you in the morning and at night, why call us at work? Learn to make it through the day without calling unless it is to say "I love you" or you are bleeding from an open wound.

- You probably don't want to know what we're thinking about. If women knew what men were really thinking about, they would be spitting on us all day every day.

Just thought you'd like to know...

Estrogen

After eighteen years of bachelorhood in between my ex-wife "Plaintiff" and my new bride "Bubba-Lishous," it has been an adjustment learning to live with a woman. I love 'Lishous, but women are all wonderfully strange creatures to me. There is this new thing called estrogen in my house now and I'm having a bit of trouble adjusting to it.

Estrogen is a medical term for "I am woman, hear me roar!" 'Lishous has these mood swings that alter my lifestyle from time to time. Some of them are fun, but I can't seem to catch the humor in all of them. Like when "everyone on Bubba's Beach has an attitude problem" but her, and she's adding jelly beans to my omelet at breakfast. I can tell the estrogen level is on the rise when she uses my cell phone to call every single company in the United States that has a truck on the road with a bumper sticker that says, "How's my driving, call 800-xxx-xxxx," and she tells them!

I usually leave the house when she starts to talk to the dog like he is human and the parrots haven't said a word in three days, they know better. I think that the estrogen level is raised by her two female cats that came with the marriage. Lots of estrogen, little defense on my part. Rolex, my dog (I named him that because he is a "watch" dog), and I are the only two males in the house and I can't shake my tail like he does to avoid the mood swings. She perceives things that amaze me... like how to interpret the expressions on her cats' faces and the difference between seventeen shades of "off-white!" To me, all my clothes are "fat clothes," not just some of them; and bean sprouts are just weeds. I don't want to eat anything that is still growing. I don't eat bean sprouts; I like my food dead. I don't think it is necessary to scream "Who is calling now?" every time the phone rings, but I do give her the phone when the telephone solicitors call. They don't ever call back!

I asked her "What's for dinner?" during the last estrogen storm, and she screamed, "Reservations!" I even tried to fix her breakfast last estrogen season, but when I asked her how she liked her eggs, she took the Midol bottle out of her mouth, glared at me with the look of Satan in her eyes, and in a voice straight out of "The Exorcist," she screamed, "UN-FERTILIZED! And that is exactly the way I intend to keep them!" God forbid we ever have a child; it would be a girl for sure, and I'd totally be outnumbered in my own home. Besides, this woman was not meant to procreate... there should be only one of this species on earth.

I asked her "What's for dinner?" during the last estrogen storm, and she screamed, "Reservations!"

When the estrogen tide comes in, I have learned to "ship out." I go somewhere, even if I don't have anyplace to go. I went to sixteen movies last week. Pray for me, I'm trying.

Just thought you'd like to know...

Sex and Higher Education

A ten-year study by the National Opinion Research Center at the University of Chicago has recently been made public. It seems that highly educated people have less sex than those that just finished high school or dropped out! Well, for the first time in my life, I am happy that I did not complete my college education. It seems that ignorance really IS bliss!

They say that high school grads average fifty-eight sexual contacts a year, while those with some college average sixty-two. If you graduated college, you only do it fifty-six times a year, and if you got a postgraduate degree, you come in last with only forty-nine times a year! Finally, a school in Chicago came up with some information that we all can really use! I know that we will all adapt this valuable information and enrich our daily lives forever!

It seems that if you work more than sixty hours a week, you have more sex than those that work forty hours or less! I can understand that. My momma always said, "The harder you work the more you get!" Also concluded was the fact that the rich do not have more sex than others. I could have told you that. The rich have far better ways to spend their free time. Someone has to play golf and ski Aspen, and you can't do those things and have sex at the same time. The most amazing thing to me is that 15 percent of the people are responsible for over 50 percent of the sexual activity, and 42 percent of adults engage in 85 percent of all sex! I guess that means that 58 percent of the sexual activity is with adults in the other 15 percent! I know that 'Lil Bubba and Bubba Jr. are doing their part, and it makes me proud to know that they are normal adults in this area! I hope that the 15 percent that are taking care of most of the sexual happenings out there are healthy and taking their vitamins, cause if they slow down we may vanish as a species!

Finally, it is said that jazz fans and gun owners are among the most sexually active Americans! Just why is that? I submit that there are more Bubbas out there than anyone ever realized before! Bubba likes jazz, as long as there is a banjo in it, and for sure owns guns. While country music may be number one, jazz is likable, and "gun control" to Bubba means that "you hit what you aim at." For once in my life I am politically correct. I am in step with society. I am in the majority. I am getting more than anyone else! God, it is great to be an American!

God bless the Bubbas of America. Where would we be without them? Just thought you'd like to know...

CHAPTER 10

The Holidays

All Bubbas love holidays. In fact, we have special ways of celebrating each and every one of them. Here are some examples of holidays celebrated "Bubba style."

Mardi Gras on Bubba's Beach

Mardi Gras is the Pagan holiday and us Baptists love it! This year's parade was better than ever. The booze held out and I got lots of new lint in my dryer for next year! However, there are a few things that must not go unnoticed about the local villagers here on Bubba's Beach. I saw things that just shouldn't be... but were allowed because it was Mardi Gras.

My friend Brian Hill, who lives right on the parade route, had so many people at his house that all the sand spurs in his yard are gone. The mainlanders took them back in the seat of their pants! I counted 43 pairs of beads on the telephone wires, and saw seven sea gulls that were trying to eat them! I saw a Pelican fly by this morning with a string hanging out his back door. He was flying rather gingerly as you might expect! I heard a drunk Masochist tell a drunken sadist, "I have some good news and some bad news... The good news is that I got bad news!" I saw a man fling himself under a car to get a pair of beads that cost 11 cents!

People were saying anything just to be heard. I heard one old man say to another one, "Now Phil, was it you who died or your brother?" I overheard a little old lady with a painted parasol say, "I'm telling you sister, I've had them both, and trust me, premature evacuation is worse!" I have no idea what they were talking about... hurricanes maybe?

I saw a lady with a T shirt that said, "Medical science has discovered a foolproof contraceptive for people over 80... Nudity!" I offered her $20 for it and she said "NO, but I'll take those red beads on your neck. And if you let me kiss you I'll give you $20." I sent the shirt to my mother. A man in the Islander bar told me that his luck was so bad that he called his 900 Phone Sex Line and the girl that answered said, "Not tonight I have an ear ache!"

This year's King of our parade, Russ Mann, served us well. He has even invented his own version of a drink called the "Pile driver." You mix equal parts Gin and Preparation H, shake well, and drink in the bathroom. Russ even looks like a king. Big head, small mouth, and beady eyes... I love him. I never found out who the queen was this year, but then with Russ as King, that is not something I would want public either! I'm not saying Russ is dull... but his birthstone is asphalt!

So Long Live the Heathens! Thanks for a great fest. I can't wait until next year when they pass out "Gas X" pills with the red beans and rice so I will be able to sleep that night!

Just thought you'd like to know...

Bubba's Steak and Sex Holiday

We here at the Bubbas of America organization have decided that it's time to create a new holiday!

It seems that women have all the holidays, except those meant for dead presidents and children. Us Bubbas just don't have a holiday... and that's a crime.

You see, every February 14 people get to display their fondness for the wife, the girlfriend, or even both by showering them with gifts, flowers, dinner, shows, jewelry, or anything else that women find romantic. I know as the head Bubba that I have to rack my brain for that one special day for "jusssst the right gift that will show my wife, Bubba-Lishous, that I really love her more than anything on earth. Even my dog Rolex has dog days named after him in the month of August! But us Bubbas ain't got nuthin'—NADA, ZIP, Zilch, not even an hour or minute, much less a day.

Father's Day don't count... what about all the Bubbas that ain't fathers?... lots of men have better sense than some of us! Did you know that AT&T states that the number one day for _collect calls_ in America has always been Father's Day? Now what does that tell you?... it just don't count!

There should be a holiday for the ladies to show their love for the men in their life. Men and most Bubbas just won't admit that they are embarrassed about this. They are either too proud or too stupid to ask for it. Well, I'm asking for it... right here and now.

I hereby declare that May 1st, every year from now on, is _Steak and Sex Day_... simple and self-explanatory! It will replace that weird German "May Day" thing that we never celebrate anymore.

This special Bubba day will be created so you ladies don't have to shop, hunt, or lose sleep... as hard as we do to choose "just the right gift." You know right up front just what to give us, and you can finally show us that you love us as much as we love you. No cards, no flowers, no bad ties, no T-shirts that we never wear, no socks, no special nights on the town, no company, no parties—just steak and sex.

I hereby declare that May 1, every year
from now on, is Steak and Sex Day...
simple and self-explanatory!

You can serve the two anyway you like; just dish it out! We don't care if the steak is rare, but we want the sex "well done," if you see what I'm saying here!

Now you got it. So get busy, and remember May 1st is Steak and Sex Day. Be there. This holiday can be celebrated alone, but it really is a holiday meant for two... or more?!!

Just thought you'd like to know...

On July the Fourth

Much has been said about the signers of the Declaration of Independence—some of it is not true, and much of it has grown into urban legend. But I'm sure these men we call "the signers" were not your typical politicians. They were signing their death warrant if found and captured by the ruling mighty British Army. I once said in a political debate that they were just a bunch of "right-wing, anti-government gun nuts that didn't want to pay their taxes," and that ain't far from the truth. But, deep down, I know they were men of means, accomplished men, gentlemen; some of them were far beyond their years in thinking, and their genius was laid out on a piece of parchment that today is the longest-standing statement of freedom in the world.

The signers realized the magnitude of what they had done, and the celebration of each anniversary retained its luster for them. Many of the signers experienced early death, but the lives of two of them were uniquely prolonged in order that they might observe the fiftieth anniversary. I always thought that it was odd that John Adams and Thomas Jefferson both died on the same day—the 4th of July. As a child I thought this was a very large coincidence, and wondered just what happened to make this a fact. I thought that maybe they were so into what they had done that they planned it out, made it happen, but they were beyond that. They were giants far above something so trivial, so I did my research and discovered these facts that I shall share with you.

Even though they grew closer in later years, John Adams and Thomas Jefferson did not like each other. They were political opposites and were constantly trying to outdo one another. In fact, they did not like each other at all... but they did respect each other. When Jefferson defeated Adams in his run for presidential reelection in 1800, Adams was so angry that he refused to stay in Washington to attend the inauguration. Twenty-six years later, when he was ninety years old, in poor health, and failing fast, the bedridden Adams was determined to hang on until July 4. At dawn on that day, when he was awakened by his attendant, Adams asked, "Do you know what day this is?" The attendant replied, "Oh, yes, it is the glorious Fourth of July. God bless it. God bless you all." I don't know who he was, but this man was living in a time that made him aware of the price that had been paid to be free. Adams then slipped into a coma. Later that afternoon, he recovered consciousness briefly and murmured, "Thomas Jefferson still survives." With these last words, he passed away, believing that Jefferson gained his final conquest over him by outliving him. Now, that is my kind of man! Even in death he was a competitor! He died thinking that the

T. Bubba (in the back) with his brothers, (left to right) Lee, Charles and Larry.

greatest accomplishment of his life was going to be celebrated by Jefferson without him around, taking all the credit!

What he did not know was that on the evening of July 3, the same year, Thomas Jefferson, age eighty-three, was also on his deathbed. He opened his eyes and whispered to a friend sitting with him, "This is the Fourth?" The friend, not wanting to disappoint the dying man, remained silent. Jefferson repeated the question. The friend nodded slightly. A smile and a look of deep satisfaction came upon Jefferson's face. He sighed, lay back, and fell into a deep sleep. He died shortly after noon on the fourth.

The news of this extraordinary happening spread quickly and a sense of reverent awe swept the country. Newspaper columns were edged in black and memorial services were held throughout the nation. Can you imagine what people must have thought? Can you believe it to this day? I can only imagine that today it would take all living presidents dying on the same day to even begin to match this extraordinary event. The fiftieth anniversary of the signing of the Declaration of Independence was indeed special.

As I sat tonight on the beach watching the fireworks over my beloved Pensacola Beach, I held my wife's hand for just a minute and thought of how very fortunate I am to have been a student of history and learned to love this country a bit differently than anyone else I know. Not any more, or any less, just differently. I have friends who laid down their lives. Even my brother Larry—a Marine who kept me out of Vietnam because he went back four times so none of his three brothers would ever have to go. I talk every day to friends on this beach that served to keep me free, and sometimes I feel so lucky that I was given this sense of history so I could appreciate what they did for me so much more.

That's what I thought about as the bombs of beauty were going off in the night sky this July 4th right here on Bubba's Beach.

Just thought you'd like to know...

The Laughing Thanksgiving at Sister Dixie's House

This year we had dinner at my sister's house in Mississippi. Her name is Dixie and as the name implies, she can cook up some Southern! It was 'bout traditional as you can get... candied yams, smoked turkey, corn bread stuffing, 'naner puddin', and three or four types of dessert I ain't got over yet. It was the first time I ever saw Bubba-Lishous eat an entire plate with nothing on it but desserts! She had one of everything on her plate and ate most of it with her eyes closed! Now, you know it is good eatin' when you eat with your eyes closed and every time someone speaks, you just ignore them with a sly smile and keep eating! I have only seen that look on her face one other time and I can't write about that here!

As we were fixing dinner, we were far enough away from Momma to get into a weird state of mind. As I unwrapped the turkey I had smoked at home, Dixie said, "My, what a huge breast!"... and that started it. Every time anyone said anything you usually hear around any holiday feast, we just busted up! Anyone who was not in the kitchen when it all started just thought we were nuts and had had our heads in the smoker when I did the turkey!

When I said, "I had to tie the turkey's legs together to keep it moist inside," I thought Sis would bust a gut; and when I said, about the thermometer on the breast, "I knew it was ready when that thing popped up," I nearly died!

When we sat down to eat, it got worse! When I cut the leg off the twenty-five-pound turkey, my brother, Larry, said, "Man, that's the biggest one I have ever seen," and we all just tried to smile, but it broke out into loud guffaws! Then when he finished he said, "If I don't unzip my pants, I'm gonna bust." I spit my yam out onto my plate or I would have choked. Then he said, with pumpkin pie in hand, "It's Cool Whip time" and I had to leave the table and go outside!

When Momma asked my brother-in-law, Junior, "Are you ready for seconds, yet?" Sister had to bury her face in her napkin and then Mom scolded one of her grandchildren with "Don't play with your meat!" We all laughed so hard we could not straighten back up! Momma thought we had lost our collective minds!

Just when we all gained a little composure, Dixie went to put an apple pie in the oven to warm it up for the ice cream and Bubba-Lishous asked "How long will it take after you stick it in?" We all just fell to the floor with our faces in our hands. That was just too much. We laughed until we cried and had to hold onto each other to remain upright! It was one of those times none of us will ever forget! If we all live long enough to have Thanksgiving dinner twenty years from now, we will have the "Laughing Thanksgiving Dinner" to remember. After all, that is what the holiday season is all about anyway... creating memories!

Just thought you'd like to know...

Holiday Eating

It is the time of the year the "Food Police" come out. Watch for them; they will be in every store you go into, every magazine you read, and every TV commercial you watch, with their annual tips on how to get through the holidays without gaining twenty pounds.

They will have "do's and don'ts" we never heard of. I say, "Shut up and go pound cauliflower in your ear!" They will tell us to eliminate second helpings, cookies with high butterfat, and gravy. What would the holiday season be without gravy? They will sing the virtues of carrot sticks. Who the hell has a favorite Christmas memory of a carrot stick? I won't buy any carrots for Christmas unless I want to feed my bird Abbub. (His name is Bubba backwards, cause he's an African Grey and Abbub sounds African to me!)

I say EAT. It is the time of the year to EAT, to DRINK, to be MERRY, and have FUN! No one ever had fun with a carrot stick!

Anyone who would put carrots, cauliflower, or turnips on a holiday buffet knows nothing of the Christmas spirit and should be flogged with a long onion! If you see carrots, leave that very moment, go somewhere they are serving rum balls and chocolate drinks that leave milk marks on your entire face!

And oh yes, drink all the eggnog you can. It will be gone next month and you won't get another shot at it for eleven months. Speaking of shots, a good single malt scotch goes well with eggnog. I know what eggs are, but I ain't discovered yet what a NOG is... but drink up anyway; it is the nectar of the Gods! Who cares that it has 1.5 million carbs per sip? You are not going to have to go to Eggnog Anonymous. Have one for me and one for every Bubba or Bubbette you know. Drink up... take a bath in it. It's later than you think!

Anyone who would put carrots, cauliflower, or turnips on a holiday buffet knows nothing of the Christmas spirit and should be flogged with a long onion!

Remember also, if anything comes with gravy, eat it. That's the entire point of gravy. Pour it on, lap it up, find something to sop with, and don't leave any on the plate, because it can dry and has been known to ruin fine china! Build a volcano of smashed potatoes and fill it with all kinds of gravy. There are things in gravy this time of year that you won't find any other time. Eat and repeat! What is Christmas dinner without gravy? It's like buying a four-wheel drive without a winch on front! You miss the entire meaning of the thing! Eat, be happy; if you don't, it causes gas.

Just thought you'd like to know...

The Christmas Dream

(This essay was written on my first ever Christmas alone. It is dedicated to all those people who may have this experience this or any year. Life is not over. Christmas is here.)

It was Christmas day. Home was far away in my mind. I kept singing "I'll Be Home for Christmas" and other songs that brought my childhood back to me. Thoughts of a cold, damp southern Mississippi, with a pine-knot fire. My brothers and mother near; and a pine tree decorated with cardboard cutouts and popcorn. There were mental pictures of family and friends, Christmas dinner, church, and just a good time. There were dreams of the Christmas day I wanted with my children around me, my dog sleeping at my feet, and the smell of a turkey smoking in the backyard.

Somehow my life never turned out to be like the dream. It was as though the past had eluded the present. Things could never be like they were, like I had dreamed them to be. Divorce, age, the "empty nest syndrome," war, fake friends, and financial mistakes had taken their toll. And to top it off, I was alone with it all.

Today was today, not yesterday.

It was this day that I knew Christmas was only a dream in the mind of what might have been. What could have been. What I wish it would be. However, the dream still exists for me. I still believe in the magic of Christmas morning. While the patter of little feet has long ago left my ears, and there is no one left to tuck into bed the night before, I still awake to a blessed day that is like no other. I know that the past really happened, but the future did not work out to be what I wanted it to be. Why, then, do I still believe as I do?

I think maybe it is because this is not the place where dreams come true. Dreams still come true in the future. The life for me is to keep striving for that dream. I must believe that the most wonderful Christmas day is yet to come. Maybe it will be this year! I hope so. I love the feeling waiting for that day gives me... that special faith and warmth that comes from knowing that Christmas day is really the birthday of Jesus. All the goodness in my world is in this day, this day of days! I must feel this way; any way else is to live less of a life... I refuse to do that.

Christmas is the promise of a better world. No Christmas will ever match the memories of yesterday. However, we can all dream, plan, and work to make this Christmas the best ever. I choose to do this. I will make my Christmas the greatest ever. I will smile, be happy for others, help someone today who needs it, wait for my sons to telephone, and remember all the joyous Christmases of my past. I will always believe in the magic of Christmas day and all it brings to me. Thank you, God, for your son; thank you for *my* sons, and for Christmas, forever!

Just thought you'd like to know...

The Christmas Hitchhiker

Yesterday, as I was coming over the three-mile bridge from the Pensacola side coming home from Christmas shopping, I passed a man walking. He had a small suitcase, he looked clean, and I did something I had not done in thirty years. I pulled over and asked him if he wanted at least a "ride across the bridge." He was not hitchhiking; he was walking, on his way to somewhere!

He looked me over, deciding whether or not he wanted to get into my Jeep with the likes of me. After a moment, he smiled and said, "Yes, that would save me what looks like a very windy walk!" I asked him where he was going and he said he was on his way to see his nine-year-old daughter, Penny, in Sarasota. He said that he hoped to reach her by Christmas Eve.

Then, I guess because I seemed interested and he had not had anyone to talk to for days, he told me the whole story of a once-happy marriage, the death of his wife (when his daughter was three), how he had "went bad" and had "done wrong" not keeping in touch with her. He had turned to drink for several years, lost his job as a computer programmer, and when he could not find work again, he had to send his little girl to live

"Little Jimmy Dickens" with T. Bubba back stage at the Grand Ole Opry.

with his brother and sister-in-law, "cause they never had any children of their own and loved her like she was theirs!"

I asked him where he lived now and he said that he had found work in construction in New Mexico, in a town called Hobbs. He said that he had been working for nearly a year, but had not been able to save enough to buy a car that would drive far enough to see his daughter! So, he decided to walk! He said he had kept to the by-ways, "cause it is against the law to hitchhike or even walk on the interstate or freeways." He had been gone for nearly a week! He said, "I have met some very nice people, got a lot of rides, slept under the stars a few times, and all in all, it has been a good trip!"

Before I got my mind on where I was going, I noticed that I was nearly in Navarre! I told him that I had to "go home" at the next bridge (the Navarre toll bridge), and asked him how much money he had. He told me that was "none of my business!" He said, "I appreciate the ride, Bubba, but I got plenty of money to make the trip. "I've been saving for this."

As I pulled off of Highway 98, I pulled out a $100 bill and told him, "I'm not giving you this money, cause you don't need it, but I want you to buy your daughter something nice from Santa Claus!" He looked at me and said, "Santa Claus don't drive no Jeep!" He smiled. I smiled and said, "If you don't take it I am going to throw it out in the highway, right now!" and rolled down my window. He took it! As he got out, he pulled out his wallet and gave me one of the three second-grade school pictures he had and told me, "Penny would like Santa to have a picture of her." I took it and framed it, and it is on my piano today to remind me that when I wear my Bubba Claus hat the entire month of December, I will stay thankful that my sons are strong and loving, and that all is right in the world, as long as I achieve the feeling I had as I drove home. It was North Pole South, and Santa Claus drove a Jeep, at least that day!

I never knew the love of a father; I never had one. Not even a bad one. I never knew the love of a man until I was married and felt that way about my father-in-law, Dr. Robert Clayton Carter. I know he loved me. However, I was no longer a child. I do not know what it means to be loved by a man as a child, but if I ever have the opportunity in another lifetime, I hope God sends me one that would walk damn near all the way across America just to see me for Christmas.

Just thought you'd like to know...

'Tween Week

Happy 'Tween? What is that, you say? It's my new holiday. Since everyone in the country is saying Happy Holidays this time of year, just to be politically correct and not step on anyone's toes, for fear that they might lose a $2 sale, I thought I'd just add a holiday!

It's 'Tween Week! Since that man out in California made up an African-American Holiday a few years back for this season, I'm making up 'Tween Week! It's the time between Christmas and New Year's Day. Those seven days that are "'tween" everything. These are days that we just don't want to work. We want to learn how to use our Christmas presents, eat leftover turkey sandwiches, watch the Bowl games, get ready to really hurt ourselves on New Year's Eve, clean out our bill drawer, get the end-of-the-year check stubs in order, enjoy the beginning of basketball season, go deer hunting, and generally do nothing! Yep, it's 'Tween Week. Why, even the folks on the job ain't working. It's time to get 'tween everything, take no sides, make no decisions, and rest up for next year.

I'm making up 'Tween Week! It's the time between Christmas and New Year's Day.

I'm going to write Congress to see if we can't make it a national holiday. Then we would have four or five holidays between Thanksgiving and New Year's Day. I say four or five, depending on what nationality you are. I think lazy folks need a holiday too! Bubbas, rednecks, lawyers, and shepherds all need to lobby for this holiday. Then we could all get together and do nothing. Maybe we could add senators as well, but then we'd have to at least make up lies, and that would take more energy than most would want to exert during 'Tween Week! Enjoy the 'Tween Season!

Just thought you'd like to know...

CHAPTER 11

World Politics

Mark Twain said once, "If you are going to be a humorist, say something serious before you sit down so everyone won't think you are a complete idiot!" Or maybe it was my Grandpa Walker. I'm not sure, but with my political background and world experiences, I would be amiss if I didn't say "something serious" within the covers of this book. The following are a few thoughts on how one Bubba feels in the post 9/11 era for those interested today and for future generations.

I'm Still Angry

In the days after the cowards of Islam bombed New York and our nation's capital, like most people, I went through every emotion I have in me... and today only anger is left. I can't cry anymore. I don't want to give any more blood; we have given enough to float a battleship. I don't want to call out for help from the entire world in our time of need; where has the rest of the world been the many times when we have needed them since this country began? I don't want to wait for the United Nations to debate this. I don't want to do anything but find the bastards that attacked our country and bomb them back into the last century where they belong. I want to make sure any country that gives these terrorists safe harbor to train and spew their filth knows that we will kill and destroy them if they aid them in the future.

I was appalled at the message from terrorists in Afghanistan that said, "We are sorry for the death of the children." Those that are guilty of having anything to do with this... I think we should drop bombs on their homes, hospitals, and cities and at the same time be asking forgiveness for it. We should level their country until nothing stands higher than a mailbox and then send a message to the survivors that "we are sorry for the death of the children!"

This is war, plain and simple. They hit first.
We didn't start it, but we can end it.

This is war, plain and simple. They hit first. We didn't start it, but we can end it. What did they think they would accomplish? If Hitler, Mussolini, and Tojo couldn't take our freedoms, do they really think *they* can? Do they really want to die in a "holy war?" I say "give them their wish." Let them go to their heaven; they have sent enough Americans to theirs. I think we should give them a different kind of "jihad," one that doesn't leave anyone to remember or honor them. When Colonel Kaddafi got out of hand under President Reagan, we didn't bomb his air bases or military compounds; we bombed his house and killed his daughter and many of his family. We didn't hear any more out of Muammar! When will we understand that is the only way to end this type of vermin?

In the words of a great Charlie Daniels song, "We might do some fussin' and fighting among ourselves, but you outside folks best leave us alone." I say, we are all angry and ready to fight this type of war, even the

Arab Americans that are also helping fill the body bags in New York. They are faceless until we give them a face, they are countryless until we give them a country, and they are going to be very dead when we find them.

Many calls came in from my sons and several of their friends. They are young people that have never felt like they feel today; have never seen our country attacked and didn't think it could happen. I have told them all what they are feeling is "patriotism." You don't have to be a soldier, carry a gun, and kill other people in foreign lands to be a patriot. You can be a patriot when the tears in your eyes turn to bile in your stomach as you watch the enemy use our own citizens as missiles to kill our people... when you know you have not prayed in a long time and you fall on your knees to your God.

You are a patriot when you get up off your knees, dry your eyes, and get as angry as I still am today, determined to "be a part of the solution to end this threat to our world."

You are a patriot when you look around for anything you can do to hasten the strikeback, to suffer any indignation, stand in any line, take any stock market fall—anything that will bring pain and suffering on the people that hurt our family and friends.

I say, "It's alright to get angry." I don't think any American ever charged into any battle in our history feeling good about what he or she had to do. I don't think any soldier ever had a positive attitude when they were under fire and killing people that wanted to kill them. I don't think there is a fireman or police officer in New York or Washington today that isn't still angry. I'm still angry, and I hope you are too.

I say, "Crank up the Enola Gay" and make a mudhole out of the country and people that attacked America. God send us a president like Harry Truman. He was not afraid to use atomic power to save his country from further death, nor did he care when he left office. Upon his exit interview, a reporter asked him, "Mr. President, did you ever regret killing all those innocent people when you dropped the bomb in Hiroshima and Nagasaki?" He pondered for only a moment and said, "No, I never did. The Joint

Chiefs told me we would lose over half a million soldiers if we had to invade that country. I saw it as a way to save all those lives!" He paused another moment and then said, "And by the way, I'm still waiting for those little yellow bastards to apologize for Pearl Harbor!" Now, *that* was the way to fight a war!

I am sure that is not politically correct, but I don't think America has ever won a politically correct war!

Just thought you'd like to know...

For Tommy

Were you personally touched by any of the terrorist attacks on America? Did you know anyone personally who died or was wounded in the attacks, or were you like most of us on 9/11—just "New Yorkers for a day!" Terrorist attacks somehow have always seemed a bit "detached" from us. We learned of them in the news and felt bad for a while, but since most of us never seemed to know anyone that personally was involved, we treated it like a plane crash in a foreign country—sad, but going about our daily lives a few moments afterwards. However, when it touches you personally, it is a special type of honor! When we know the person who died, it touches us forever. My best friend was one of those people.

Do you remember picking up *Time* and *Newsweek* on October 13, 1993, and seeing the dead body of a U.S. Army sergeant. being dragged through the streets of a village in Somalia? Do you remember being outraged that any country we were trying to help would do such a thing to one of our soldiers? I do. I waited to see how then-President Bill Clinton would get the Muslim war lord, Aidid, and bring him to justice, telling the rest of the world that we would never stand for this. I'm still waiting!

Well, my friend knew that young sergeant and knew him well. She grew up with him in a small town, went to high school with him, and rebuilt cars with him. The last night he was in America, he spent with her and her brothers at her apartment. They had fun, drank, and stayed up almost until dawn talking, laughing, and growing up. The young sergeant talked of his love of country, why he joined the Army, and how proud he was to be going to Somalia to feed starving people and "stand tall for America." The next time my friend saw him, he was a headless torso being dragged through the streets of a village, his corpse being beaten even more by the people he went there to feed.

The television was riveting! She was astounded. She called all her friends at once and they learned together, yet one at a time, that it was indeed their friend, Thomas Joseph Field... Tommy to them. Not Tommy— not smiling, happy-go-lucky, proud, and patriotic Tommy. How could this be? She screamed, and then she cried.

Oh, the vice-president came; the entire small town turned out for the funeral, and the flag off his casket was given to his mother and his dad, the local high school hockey coach. They prayed, did a twenty-one-gun salute, and put Tommy in the ground. All the major networks and written press interviewed the townspeople. It was a major press opportunity for many. Then they all went home, leaving the town with only the memory of Tommy and his friends.

But those people in that small town of Lisbon, Maine, will forever be touched by terrorism and represent a special kind of patriotism. They will understand it better than most of us, because they knew Tommy. We can only try to feel what they felt on September 11. We can't feel it; all we can do is try.

Maybe you know my friend—Sgt. Field's friend and the girl he "left behind" the last night of his freedom in America. She is a local DJ on our island. The one with the big smile and the eternal positive attitude; the one that moved here from Lisbon. The lady that now keeps Bubba's Beach singing and dancing. The love of my life... Ms. Tarsha Marie Ramich, aka "Lishous."

She, more than most of us, knows this new special kind of war, this terrorism, this evil that must be stopped this time. She lost her friend Tommy and she's still angry about it. I don't blame her. I'm angry too, but not like her. I can only see that she has a friend to lean on this time. I can only hold her and tell her that it will be different this time and pray that this president will not grow weary or weak or try to bring about a political end to this one. I can only hope we end it this time and end it forever.

For Tommy... for America.

Just thought you'd like to know...

Apology for the Middle East

I have pondered the Iraqi prisoner abuse scandal at Abu Ghraib and I've decided to speak my piece. To begin with, many Arabs and Muslims are asking for an apology. Here is mine!

We don't owe you anything at this point in time, NOTHING! Not one word of apology, not from me. I have seen worse abuse at college frat initiations. Pointing at a naked man, making them pile up, and taking their photos is not the same as American bodies hanging from bridges, not even close! We at the Bubbas of America are sorry that we ever took up arms and sent our young men and women to defend the Muslim world, as in Bosnia, Kosovo, Gulf War, Kuwait, and all the others who have never said "thank you" properly.

We are sorry that you have *yet* to condemn the events of 9/11 in a loud voice that would at least make us aware that you are not happy about it. After all, the murderers and cowards of 9/11 were Islamic Arabs. I am sorry that you can't see the difference between freedom that was given to you with our blood and the murderers that are your leaders, that kill you and squander your wealth. I am sorry that you can't seem to stand on your own two feet and won't take up arms against your own kind, your own people, but you want us to keep sending our sons and daughters.

I am sorry that your educational system teaches children to hate the "infidel" and that it is honorable to kill all that do not believe as you do. I am sorry that you consider me an "infidel;" I asked one of your holy men and was told that I was just that! I am sorry that you are sending your terrorists to America into your mosques to plan your attacks on the very country that gave you the freedom to do just that! I am sorry that you have taken our money in the billions to support your poverty-stricken countries and the wealthy among you continue to blame the U.S. for all their problems. I am sorry that you happened to be born on the richest oil deposits on the planet and your own leaders have taken it for themselves and left the common people to suffer. That is your way of government that allowed that to happen, not ours. Maybe the law you have that pays homicide bombers' families for the evil things they do should be stricken from your way of life, and your government may improve.

I am sorry that you have to take videos of beheadings of innocent people to wage your type of war against people that are trying to help you rebuild your country. I am sorry that your own religious Muslim extremists have killed more Arabs than any other group sent there to liberate you from their way of life. I am sorry as well that we have people like Michael Moore in our country that can make over $100 million on an untrue documentary film that causes you to believe that we are weak and in turmoil amongst ourselves. Hell, I'm sorry that Michael Moore is even an American. He is a big fat, ugly, lying wart on our butts, but don't believe him, or you will surely come to discover that we still have a Harry Truman in our political system that will get his guts up one day and drop a bomb on your entire country that will make it the kitty litter box of the world.

I'm sorry also that I have to write something like this to get it out of my system, but I'm very proud to live in a country that will allow me to do it, print it, and distribute it.

We will overcome this insult you have asked us for. When I saw that some countries were demanding an apology, I thought to myself... What!? We sent our best and our brightest to die for you and you want us to apologize for making fun of a few prisoners? I don't think so. Ask the prisoners if they would have rather been through what they have been through or hunted down and killed like the others that were with them. You may change your mind. I'm not proud of what I saw on the news, but Mr. Arab Country, I sure don't feel that we owe you a single word of apology, other than the above.

As a matter of fact, if hooking up one prisoner-of-war's genitals to a car battery will save one American soldier's life in Iraq, I have two things to say: Red is positive and black is negative! Crank it up!

Just thought you'd like to know...

It's a Weird World

I've been doing some research lately. I like research; it's the truth and it is often very funny. Someone once said, "The truth will set you free." I have no idea of what that means, but I like it! Here are some true things about the world we live in and some observations:

In Lebanon, men are legally allowed to "get frisky" with animals, but only female animals. Now this is homophobia in the worst way. Having a romantic session with a male animal is punishable by death! Man, that's a weird law, but then they are "different" from us! I don't even want to think about this any longer.

A law from the Muslims bans one from looking at "certain parts" of a corpse. Even undertakers must cover "that certain part" of a corpse with a brick or a piece of wood at all times. A brick? A piece of wood? What's wrong with a towel or a small cloth? But, I guess that they prefer to wear towels and cloth around their heads and not any other part of their body.

The penalty for "self-pleasure" in Indonesia is decapitation! Wow, now that's much worse than going blind! These people need to lighten up and "get out" more! It's cool, but it's not worth losing your head over!

In Hong Kong, a betrayed wife is legally allowed to kill her adulterous husband, but may only do so with her bare hands; but the husband's lover, on the other hand, may be killed in any manner desired! Now folks, the little woman here would have to be a 200th-degree black belt in Kung Fooie to kill him with her bare hands, but if she can do it, she can get away with it; but the "other woman" can be killed in any way she wants to kill her. I would opt for beating her to death with a wet goat... That would take a long time and hurt a bunch!

In Liverpool, England, topless saleswomen are allowed, but only in tropical fish stores!

In Liverpool, England, topless saleswomen are allowed, but only in tropical fish stores! Okay, let's examine this. First of all, anyone that would live in a town named after a pool of liver deserves to be English, but how do you reckon the tropical fish stores got this law passed just for them? Can't you see it now, "I would like to see a clown fish and a topless clerk!" That must have been one gassed customer, but look what he accomplished!! I wonder what I could see if I carried a dead mullet with me into a bar here on the Redneck Riviera?

In a study out of Auburn University, it has been discovered that if you bang your head against a wall for one hour, you can burn 150 calories! I wonder who this volunteer was? I bet it was the running back that fumbled the ball on the goal line against LSU last year.

The University of Miami has discovered that dolphins and humans are the only animals that have sex for pleasure. Now wait a minute. How did they get these two together to discover this fact? However, it may explain why we are also the only animals that can smile!

While we are at this animal thing, we know now that turtles can breathe through their butts—and you thought *you* had bad breath sometimes!

And finally, there are men in Guam whose full-time job is to travel the countryside and deflower young virgins, who pay these men for the privilege of "making whoopee" with them for the first time. I'm not making this up; it's the truth. The reason is because under Guam law, it is expressly forbidden for virgins to marry. Now I gotta ask you, is this a great job or what? Where does one get a degree in this profession? I want to register. I don't even care if they have a football team! I mean, really, do you think that these men are ever late for work, call in sick, retire, or even care if they have a benefit package? I don't think so. This must be the greatest job in the world!! Yep, it's a weird world and I'm a happy Bubba!

Just thought you'd like to know...

I'm Moving to Mexico

It is hard for me to understand people rioting in protest with Mexican flags and wanting driver's licenses and welfare.

Have we come to this? Do we really want to give people status that pledge allegiance to another flag? The lie we are all being fed about them doing cheap labor that citizens here won't do is just that, a big FAT lie.

I know illegals who moved here without becoming citizens who make over $70,000 a year and do it every year. I even know one who makes well over $100,000, pays no taxes, no workers' compensation, no social security, and has not even worried about his green card for years. I'm not making this up!

I think I'm going to move to Mexico. It's a great country, rich in natural resources, great bird hunting, beautiful seashores filled with history, and I can live there cheap. I'm going to skip all that stuff about visas, passports, and immigration laws, like they do when they come here. I'm going to demand free medical care, demand that all government forms be printed in English, not worry about learning the language, and demand that my kids are taught by English-speaking teachers.

I'm going to forget about insuring my car, my house, and my children. I'm going to demand that the month of May be Caucasian History Month in all schools and colleges. I'm going to fly my American flag on a flagpole outside my house with the Mexican flag down under it. I'm going to demand free lunches for all Caucasian children whose parents don't work, regardless of how much money they are worth.

I'm going to demand that I work two hours a day picking cactus out of the rights-of-way on the freeway, because they don't like to do that themselves down there. I'll protest for a better job once I get there and decide that I don't like the job I went there to do. I won't pay any income taxes, and I'm sure the labor laws there won't apply to me as a citizen that came to do work they don't like to do. I would demand my right to a fair trial and expect to be "innocent until proven guilty." I also will demand my right to air conditioning, because of my advanced age and color. Every time a cop stops me, I'm going to act like I can't speak Spanish, and demand my "rights" as a foreign citizen. I'm going to expect all those people to treat me like a Mexican just because I'm in their country! I'm not going to worry about the economy or what millions of people like me do to their healthcare plan. Why, I'm entitled!

WAKE UP! I'm just dreaming... How long do you think I or any American citizen would last in Mexico with that attitude? Do you think that the Mexican president would welcome millions like me? Do you think that he would still be buddies with our president? I'm sure I'd be strung up and used for a piñata about the second month, thrown in jail, and deported back to America within a short time. Why, I'd most likely be found dead among the cacti on the freeway.

Come on, Congress, where do you think this is leading us? Did we bleed and die for 200 years to build this nation just to give it away to anyone that comes here under the guise of wanting to work? I say we welcome anyone that wants to work in time of disaster to clean up, harvest crops, and do work that areas don't have people available to hire, but when that is over, go home to your native country until you decide to come to America and honor her, by first learning to speak English, pay your fair share, become a citizen no matter how hard it is, and be thankful for the opportunity to better your life. Go home until you adapt the "Ellis Island attitude" of our forefathers for all these many years. This is the attitude this nation was built on, and you are NOT welcome under any other pretenses.

Until we all adapt this attitude, we are going to lose what our ancestors gave us. It worked for as long as we have been a nation; why change it? Are we that weak of a people? Will we rise up and tell Congress they are wrong, or just sit here and let political correctness give our America away?

Just thought you'd like to know...

CHAPTER 12

★ ★ ★

Hurricanes

Recently, we have lived through two devastating hurricanes here in the heart of the Redneck Riviera. Bubba's Beach was hit by two major storms just ten months apart, Hurricanes Ivan and Dennis. So you can

This is what hurricanes do to houses on Bubba's Beach in northwest Florida.

appreciate it, remember that the Christmas tsunami was just a twenty-one foot-high wave; we recorded a *fifty-two-foot wave* just ten miles south of my island in Hurricane Ivan. This is a fact, you can look it up. We were devastated. I lost my home in Ivan and rebuilt it after ten long months of living in FEMA trailers, motor homes, and with friends. We moved back into our newly constructed home in July 2005, lived in it for twenty-one days, and Hurricane Dennis came and destroyed it again. We moved back into a second newly rebuilt home just a few months into 2006. We did not have a home to live in for almost two years and felt lucky because so many people lost so much more. Florida had eight major hurricanes in nineteen months. We were literally in hurricane hell. Why did I rebuild here? Why did I go through all of this? It is simple, but most folks don't understand it... I love where I live. If you have ever been here, you would not ask me to explain. Besides, where do you live to avoid "natural disasters?" I have the choice of fires, mud slides, earthquakes, floods, tornadoes, and hurricanes. I'll take a hurricane every time. You gotta be stupid to die in a hurricane. You have a week's notice. You can watch it on TV for five days because it is slow moving. Just get out, move to high ground and ride it out. You can't do that with the other choices. We are tough folk here on Bubba's Beach! I'm rebuilding everytime. If your gonna be stupid you gotta be tough. We are tough fold here on Bubba's Beach.

Just thought you'd like to know...

The Things We Lose

In times of loss from hurricanes, we often ponder on what we "lose." After Hurricane Ivan took nearly everything I had, it seemed to me that this "loss" thing I'm having to deal with in both my insurance and my life has come into a different perspective.

I think that when you worry too much about losing something, you've already lost it, for your worry prevents you from receiving any value out of whatever you're so worried about losing. See what I'm saying here?

Things do change, and what is here today may well be gone tomorrow. You can worry and fret over that reality, or you can joyfully and lovingly make the most of all you have right now. I choose to live in the moment. I want to enjoy what I have left, for you cannot ever again enjoy what you had.

The fact that a hurricane was the cause of my loss can hurt as well, but if I don't get over it, I just hurt inside. I don't want to hurt anymore, I want to move on. I want to be happy with my new "stuff" and again learn to enjoy life.

The joy that you fully experience, you will not lose. The love that you live and give cannot be taken from your heart by any outside circumstance.

I have found that our families and loved ones do not make our lives worth living, but loving them does. Even death cannot take that away! When we lose someone due to death, that doesn't mean we stop loving them. When I lose a loved one, I still try to live up to what they thought I was, to be better because of their influence on me, to live up to what they expected of me. I don't stop living or loving just because of they are no longer with me.

Life is habits. First we make our habits, then our habits make us. Our habits are things that people judge us on, not the things we think they judge us on. Habits are our lives to others.

If you invest yourself too heavily in the fleeting and superficial things in life, you'll be setting yourself up for a shattering disappointment when those things are no longer with you. Instead, learn to treasure those real, substantial, meaningful things that time and events cannot erase. Things like real love and ice cream!

Get in the habit of fully living each day with meaning and purpose. You'll find yourself worrying less about what you have to lose, and focusing more on what you have to use.

Express gratitude for all you have by making the very most of it, and you'll always have plenty to be thankful for. It's not what we gain in life that makes a life worth living; it's the things we lose that make us what we are. When we lose bad habits like smoking, being harsh, yelling at everything first, and not listening to those who love us most, it is then who we become what we want to be. So lose something today that will make you a better person, parent, or friend. Hurricanes be damned!

Just thought you'd like to know...

"Disposable Homes"

I have come to the conclusion that if you live near the water here on the Redneck Riviera, from New Orleans to Panama City, Florida, you live in a disposable home! I don't care what it is made out of and how much it cost; it is disposable and we need to adjust to that if we want to live in paradise!

I have now lost everything I owned in five hurricanes—Hurricane Camille on the Mississippi Gulf Coast in 1969, Hurricanes Erin and Opal in 1995, Hurricane Ivan in 2004, and Hurricane Dennis in 2005. Of course, in 1969 I was married only two years and we took a total loss and were out about $425!! This last time it was a lifetime of "stuff!" Baby pictures,

"Bubba Junior"—James Terryl Bechtol, Jr.

videos of my sons' touchdowns, a beautiful sunset with a special lady I can never forget, and Bubba, Jr. and Little Bubba surfing with a background of red sky that made me cry every time I watched. I saved some clothes and my eating utensils, my bike, cars, and the dog's bed. My sailboat made it through fine, and that is good, cause that is where I had to live for awhile! Ironic, ain't it? The boat is fine and the house is gone!

But then, that is what hurricanes and such are all about. Don't try to make any sense out of it; there is none! God gets mad every now and then and smacks us in the face to remind us of what is important in life and what is not!

Okay, God, I hear you! I had too much "stuff" and you took it! Thanks for reminding me that I don't need that much to be happy! Thanks for showing me just who my friends really are and thanks for just sending a little hurricane instead of a category five storm that would have left my island a sandbar, clean and white and totally void of any life at all! Thank you for showing me that all we have is "disposable!"

So, what do I do now? I rebuild, I get over it, I have something else to tell my grandkids one day—the thing will get worse every year, and by the time I am seventy years old, it will be the worst hurricane in the history of the world! I love living here. I will accept the bad with the good. I will not live anywhere else. I choose to live in Paradise and I will. So, there, God, until you take me, you can continue to take my "stuff." I will get more; that is what life is all about.

It is not how many times you get DOWN in life that counts; it is how many times you get UP!

Just thought you'd like to know...

Comedy Is "Tragedy Plus Time"

Steve Allen once said a long time ago that comedy is "tragedy plus time!" I learned much from my personal tragedies with life-changing hurricanes over the years... and now that some time has passed it's time to reflect on these lessons and enjoy the comedy in it all.

I have learned that:

- The voluntary all-way stop without a stoplight is the kindest thing one can do when driving.

- Military men with machine guns can run an intersection better than anyone else!

- Wet sand is the heaviest thing in the world!

- Radio is the best way to watch television.

- When I rebuild my house, my closets are going to have lots of leg room.

- There are no B cell batteries, and I don't know why we skipped the B's.

- A man with a chainsaw that shows up at your front door is not necessarily a scary thing.

- SUVs are the best tents for sleeping in on the market today. Everyone should have one!

- Your washing machine can be used as a cooler, and the dryer is good for a cat house.

- It's okay to sit on your own back steps, cook on your grill, and eat in your underwear.

- We actually do need to buy a generator, no matter how hard it is to store the rest of the time.

- The best word in priceless is ICE!

- If gasoline goes to $20 a gallon, it's still worth it.

- Cell phones are the greatest invention of mankind; it is now beyond the computer.

- My wife is even more beautiful in candlelight!

- Air conditioning is the greatest invention of mankind, beyond the cell phone!

- Six-day-old potato chips are not all that bad!

- If you cook any meat long enough over an open fire, you can cook the "bad" out of it.

- Buildings will be totally blown away, but the political sign in the front yard will still be standing.

- The best diet I have ever been on is an empty refrigerator.

- Going to an air-conditioned, dark movie house to see anything is a great night out!

- Getting back to your home can be the most important thing in your life, even if you know that it is going to be the very worst of news.

The best diet I have ever been on
is an empty refrigerator.

- And finally, I learned that people love me that I didn't know before this tragedy, and me them!

Just thought you'd like know...

What Amazes Me

I lost my home twice to hurricanes in less than a year. When that happens, amazing things become apparent. I am amazed...

That the Indian Ocean tsunami was only a twenty-one-foot tidal wave and we recorded a <u>fifty-two-foot</u> wave just off of Bubba's Beach. Engineers said it was still forty feet high when it took out the Interstate 10 bridge—that is *fourteen miles* inland! It is the only way I can explain to all those who ask me questions about the hurricanes when I travel. It is the first time they are able to put it into perspective what we have suffered through!

At how a small pile of rubble in the front of your house was once your entire home and all of its contents!

That our beach is still beautiful, even with the piles of trash that used to be homes and businesses.

That I can hear the gulf side of the island on the sound side for the first time ever. There is nothing left to break that beautiful sound—no sand dunes, no homes, no streets, no lamp posts, nothing. It is a sad sound.

At how big the sky is without the normal light pollution that blocks the stars and leads the Loggerhead turtles astray when they lay their eggs. The night sky is as big as Montana's.

That people I have never spoken to nod and smile when they see me.

That I have learned to live in a mobile home with a two-foot-wide refrigerator, I can sleep in a bunk bed an elf wouldn't fit into, and how to watch 788 satellite channels on a thirteen-inch TV screen!

That I'm going to church in a hotel, my dog has learned to live on a chain, and my wife has learned to cook over a candle!

That so many people have learned that "less is really more." We have learned that we just don't need all that "stuff" that is gone with the wind, to be happy.

And finally, while living in an RV while our house was being rebuilt, we were saying things that we never thought we'd ever say—such as, "Honey, we have a flat tire on the house!" And recently we left for a short trip and as we were leaving 'Lishous said, "Honey, did you unplug the house?" Amazing!

Just thought you'd like to know...

About T. Bubba Bechtol

T. Bubba Bechtol, from Pensacola Beach, Florida (aka, Bubba's Beach), has become one of the nation's funniest observers of human nature simply by calling it like he sees it. Whether it's entertaining audiences on television talk shows, performing in concert halls, or doing his standup routine at the Grand Ole Opry, T. Bubba has earned a reputation as a down-to-earth humorist. His quick wit crosses all regional, gender, generational, and class lines. T. Bubba's debut CD on MCA Nashville, *I'm Confused* (recorded live at the Pensacola Little Theater during two sold-out performances), captures his ability to meld a Southern accent with humorous insights that make everyone laugh—regardless of where they call home. T. Bubba's routines draw as much from the comedic insights of Jerry Seinfeld and Bill Cosby as from Minnie Pearl and Jerry Clower.

You can visit T. Bubba and listen to his humor at his Web site, www.TBubbaFun.com.

T. Bubba started out in life as James Terryl Bechtol, a baby boomer raised in the tiny fishing village of Fountainbleau, in the heart of Mississippi's Cajun country. "We lived so far in the woods we had to walk toward town to hunt," he quips. His mother, a Marine veteran, provided tough love, guidance, and a sense of humor. His grandfather, a circuit-riding Southern Baptist minister, exposed Bechtol to oral tradition. At ten, Bechtol was preaching at tent revivals up and down the Gulf Coast. "I broke away from that when I got to high school and discovered Jack Daniels and cheerleaders," he says.

A star athlete in his high school years, Bechtol received a scholarship to play football at Perkinston College in Wiggins, Mississippi. After an injury, he transferred to the University of Southern Mississippi his junior year. However, he says there was one course he was looking for that wasn't in the curriculum catalog: "How to make money." When he couldn't find that course listed, he left college.

Bechtol left formal education to pursue a career in direct sales. He found his natural sense of humor gave him the ability to talk to anybody about anything, whether it was selling home fire alarm systems or tanning beds. (Yes, Bechtol was the guy who first imported Wolf Tanning Systems from Germany to the South.) His career skyrocketed, enabling the young entrepreneur to sell his business and retire by his fortieth birthday. Along the way, he built a national network of contacts that remembered his leadership skills as well as his laughs. In 1980, he was elected president of the United States Jaycees, the first Southerner to hold the job in decades.

The stint led to a brief career in politics. In the '80s, Bechtol moved to Washington, D.C., to join the Ronald Reagan camp as a fundraising director. He worked for two years in the Reagan White House and then ran for office himself as a candidate for congressman in Florida's Congressional District 1. He won the primary but lost the general election.

Looking at the crossroads of his future, Bechtol heard his phone start to ring. People were calling to see if he would serve as a speaker at various functions. Soon, the one-time salesman-turned-politician found himself in high demand as a motivational speaker at conferences, conventions, and industrial events. One quality made him stand out from most on the rubber-chicken-dinner circuit: Bechtol was funny. Side-splittingly funny.

At this time, he began reflecting on a job he had as a teenager he calls "the greatest influence on my comedy career." In those summers back on the Gulf Coast, Bechtol worked as a driver for the brashly outrageous standup comic, "Brother" Dave Gardner. Gardner, whose regional shtick included jokes about "RC Colas" and "Moon Pies," had gone from regional clubs to frequent appearances on "The Tonight Show." Bechtol spent a great deal of time with the comedian, driving him around town during gigs in Biloxi. "What makes people laugh has fascinated me my whole life," he says. "I was buying comedy tapes when kids my age were buying music. Brother Dave made me realize I could do it as a profession."

After 35 years in the National Speakers Association as one of the nation's top humor speakers, Bechtol developed a friendship with another humorist, syndicated columnist Lewis Grizzard. Taken with Bechtol's bluntly transparent view of life, Grizzard began writing about "Bubba" in his books and columns in the Atlanta *Journal-Constitution*. When Grizzard's health problems became severe, he asked T. Bubba to serve as a substitute for personal appearances he was not able to make. "He was a huge influence on me," Bechtol says of the late writer. "He gave us all permission to be both smart—and be Southern."

With a growing reputation as a standup comic, Bechtol was taken under the wing of Grizzard's management company, which began booking him on comedy dates. He was spotted by former talk show hosts Charlie Chase and Lorianne Crook, who booked him on The Nashville Network's "Music City Tonight." In his first year on the program, Bechtol appeared more than fifty times and became immensely popular with country music audiences. Impressed with his talents, Opryland Productions recruited Bechtol to host a musical review called "Boots, Boogie & Blues" at the Governor's Theater in Pigeon Forge, Tennessee. He made his first appearance on the Grand Ole Opry on October 24, 1998, and has performed there regularly ever since. In the summer of 2001, Bechtol became one of the few standup comics in the nation to receive a major recording contract when he was signed to MCA Nashville resulting in his top selling comedy album *I'm Confused.*

What does he consider the key to his appeal?

"I can be funny without having to use words or actions others resort to," he says. "You can repeat my jokes at work on Monday in front of anyone—even at church. Besides, I've had to keep my comedy clean, because my momma's still alive. If I didn't, she'd whoop me good still today!"

Hey Y'all...

I dun hooked up to the Internet!
Come visit me at:

TBubbaFun.com

We'll have a
good time...

Just because you
bought this book, you
get a **Secret Bubba Password**
to use at the Web Site:

298982

Come check it out!

And listen... thanks for buying
my book.